Colorist Palette Reference Book

Test and Chart Your Favorite Color Combinations

By Ligia Ortega
ColoringPress.com

This book is dedicated to Cindy N. Thank you so much for sharing your gorgeous colored pages and most of all for the caring, encouragement, and kindness you show.

Artist's Message

It means so much to me that you have chosen to purchase my book. Thank you from the bottom of my heart for your support of my work. I hope it helps make trying new color combinations more fun, and that it helps make your favorite color palettes easy to find for future reference.

All line art in this book was hand drawn by me. I also sourced, restored, and processed the grayscale images to make them colorable. I then worked to digitize every page and assembled them electronically to prepare for printing. This coloring book is a tangible representation of my time and work. I took the time and additional expense to officially register this book with the Copyright Office. Please respect Copyright Law.

You may:

- Copy the uncolored pages on other paper preferences for yourself.
- Post colored images on social media.
- Give the colored pages as a gift.
- Use the physical colored pages for cards or bookmarks.
- Those cards and bookmarks may be given as gifts.
- Give a physical book you purchased as a gift.

You may not:

- Share physical or electronic copies of uncolored pages with anyone else, whether free or for sale.
- Post uncolored pages anywhere online, claim them as your own, or distribute uncolored pages via e-mail or electronic downloads.
- Incorporate uncolored or colored images on items besides colored pages, bookmarks, and cards.
- Sell uncolored or colored images, cards, or crafts made with the coloring pages, use them on products, or for any commercial usage.

Copyright © 2017 Ligia Ortega. All rights reserved. I am grateful for your support of artist/author's rights.

In accordance with the U.S. Copyright Act of 1976, the scanning, uploading, and electronic sharing of any part of this book without the permission of the artist/author constitutes unlawful **piracy** and **theft** of the artist/author's intellectual property except for the provisions above. Coloring any image does not transfer copyright or any rights to you, nor does it create a new copyright in your name. If you would like to use material from the book, prior written permission must be obtained by contacting the artist/author at:

ColoringGifts@yahoo.com   ColoringPress.com   www.facebook.com/ColoringPress

ISBN: 978-1975926069

ISBN: 1975926064

How to Use This Book

While working on my latest book *Coloring Gifts™: Gifts of Friendship* I was coloring a page for the cover and decided to try a different color combination than my usual ones. I tend to have coloring palette ruts, I generally stick to my usual favorite color combinations - and although I admire other people's colored pages that venture into other palettes, when it comes time to color, I tend to stick with the same "safe" colors for the most part. So here I am a couple hours into this page with these very uncomfortable new colors and need to pick two or three more colors to finish. And I start getting nervous. What if the new colors won't work? I'd have to start over and this book is so late in being published as it is. I opened my graphics program, scanned the page and roughly tried several other colors and finally found a few that worked. It took a long time to scan and crudely try these colors - hoping I had pencils and markers that matched what I was seeing on the screen.

Aside from the fact that this could have been easily prevented by, you know, picking my colors ahead of time (something I never seem to do... I generally color on the fly, choosing colors as I go along!) I told myself I really could have used a way to swatch these colors or try them somewhere else to see how they worked together. The idea bugged me for a couple of weeks until this morning when it all came together. I sometimes have colorists ask what colors I used for certain pages and I usually forget because I keep my pencils stored in the same color order and I put them all away when I finish a page. So I could also use some way to help me keep track of color combinations used in pictures I've colored. Plus if I can't finish a picture in one sitting, this book would help me keep track of pencils and markers I have used so I can put things away without forgetting what colors I was using. A book where I could test new coloring techniques, and try different, scary new palettes on a small scale. Turns out that a book like this one would be very useful! So I set out to put one together.

This book has 48 pages with pages in 12 different designs: a color wheel, some abstract designs, some flowers, some doodles, even a couple small grayscale images. Below each design there are 12 different blocks for you to swatch or blend the media you use (markers, pencils, gel pens, etc.) and a line to write what the colors and media are used next to it. There is also additional room for notes above and below the lines. The designs are small and they do not have to be fully colored: they are there for you to color as much or as little as you want - the purpose is to test colors to see how they work together or to keep a record of different media and color combinations you have used.

The pages are all single sided so you can use a variety of media, including alcohol markers. Just be sure to slip either some cardstock or a few pages to prevent bleed through or indentations from pencils or gel pens.

Thank you so much for your purchase - I hope you enjoy the book!

Ligia Ortega

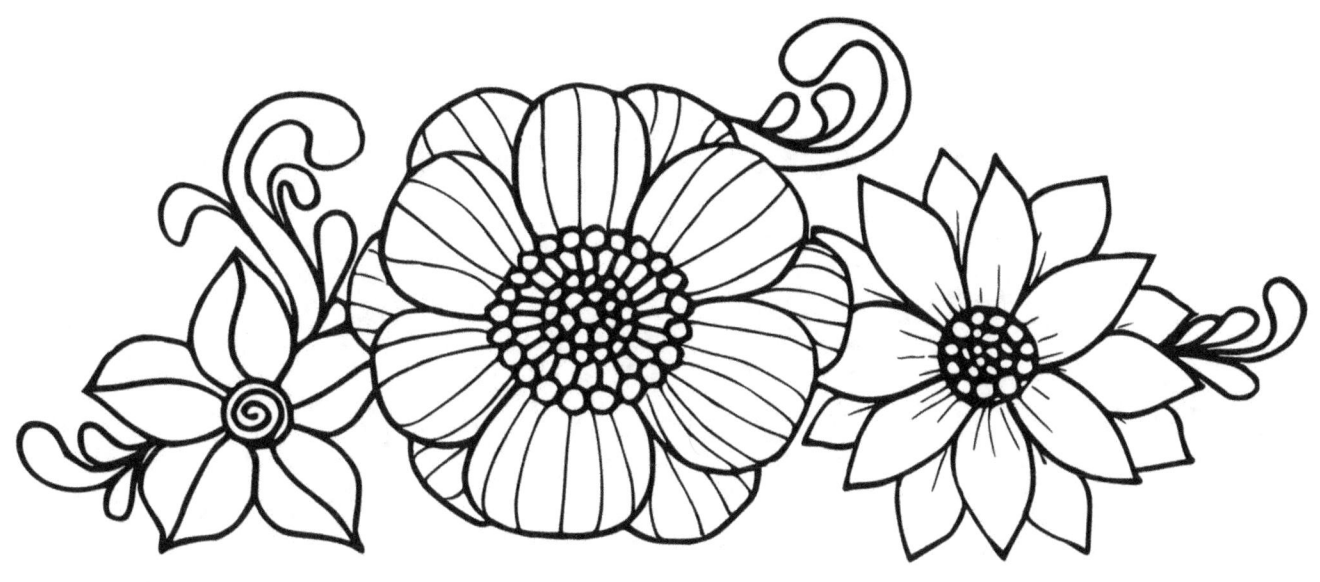

Colorist Palette Reference Book © Ligia Ortega - ColoringPress.com

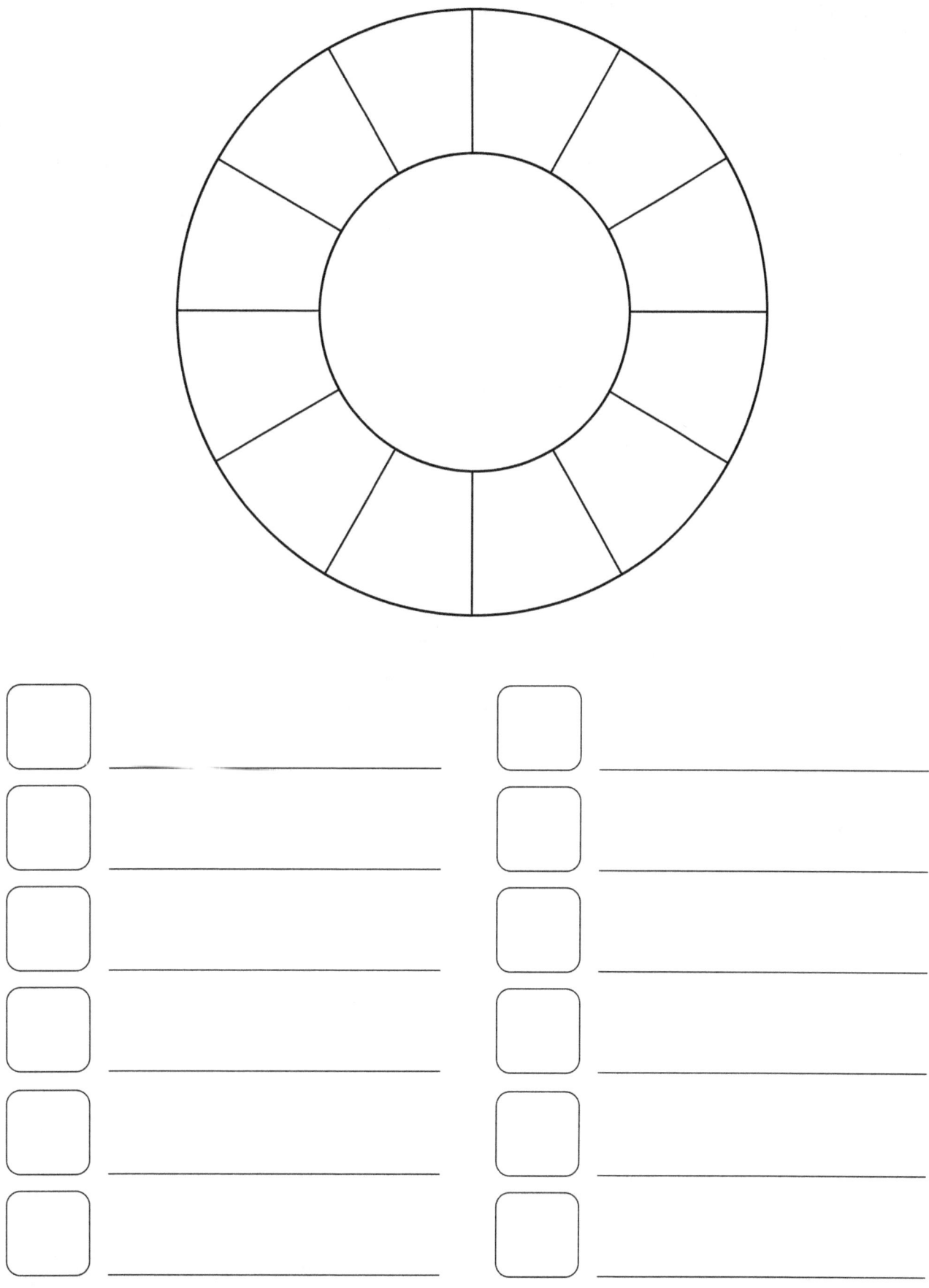

Colorist Palette Reference Book © Ligia Ortega - ColoringPress.com

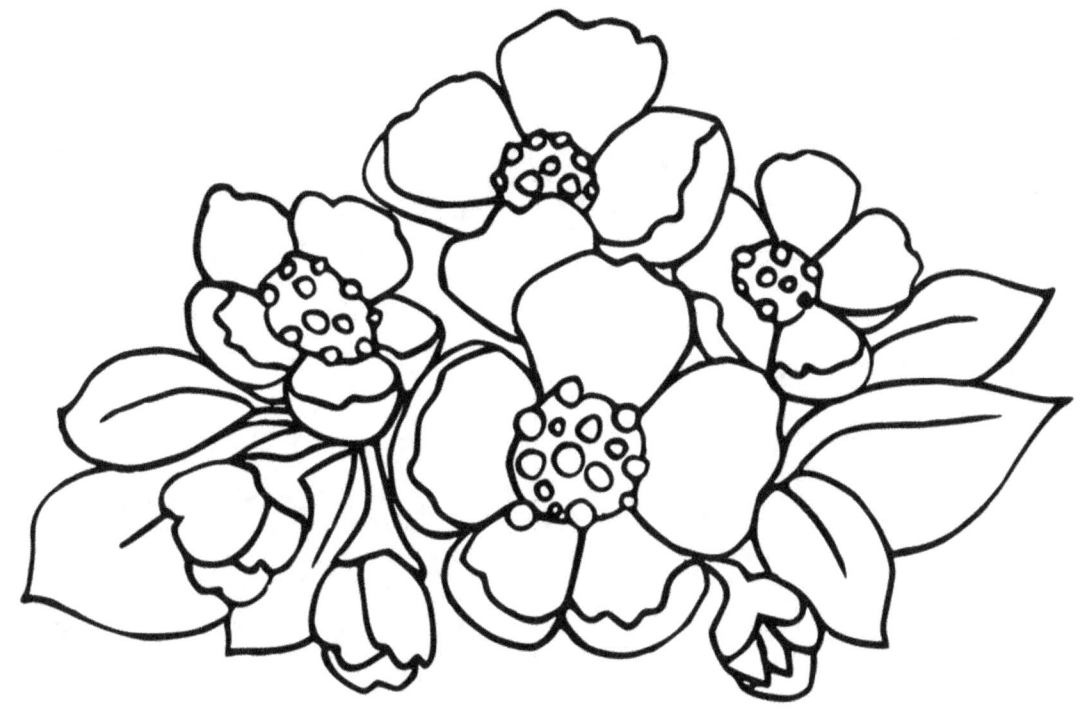

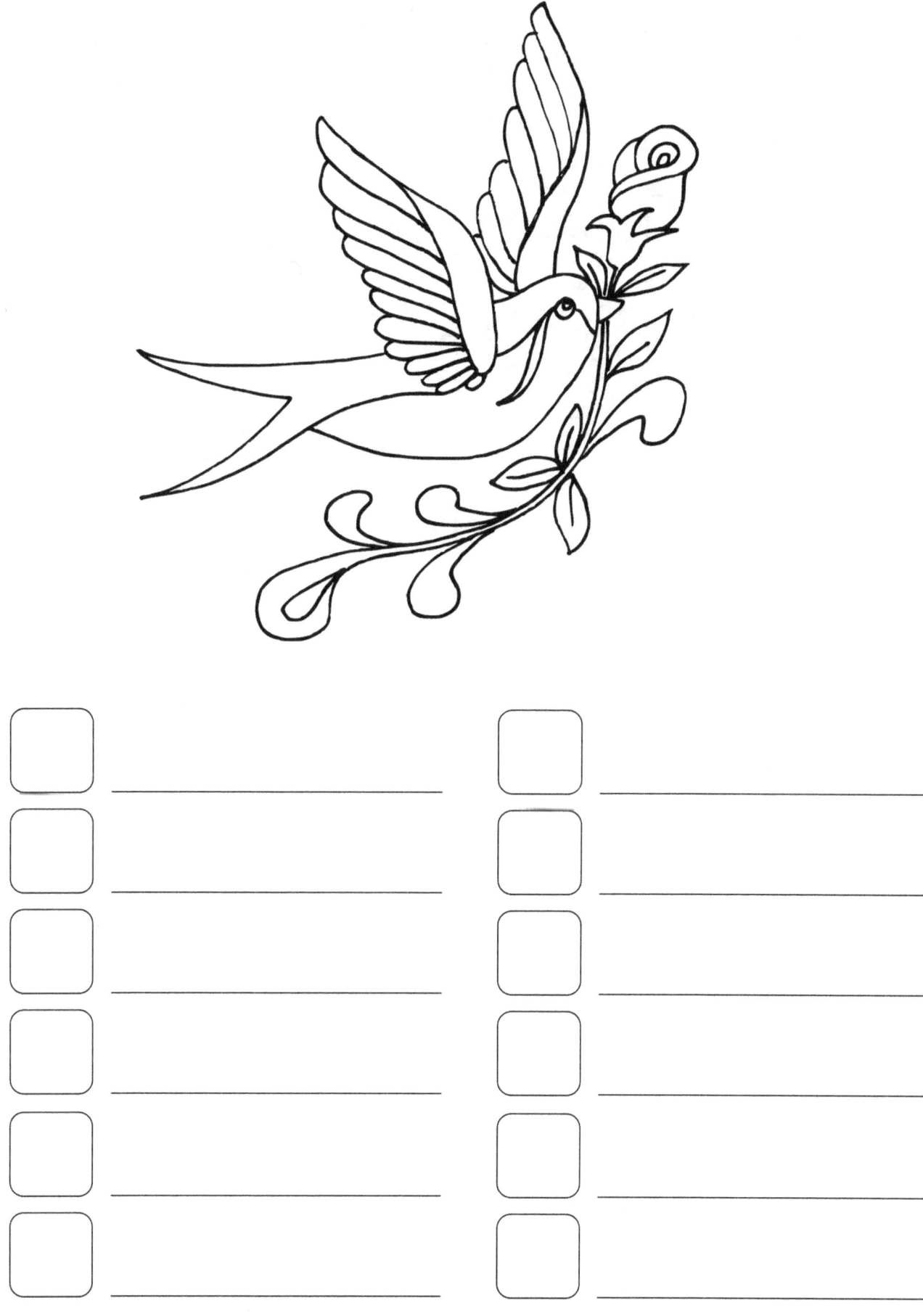

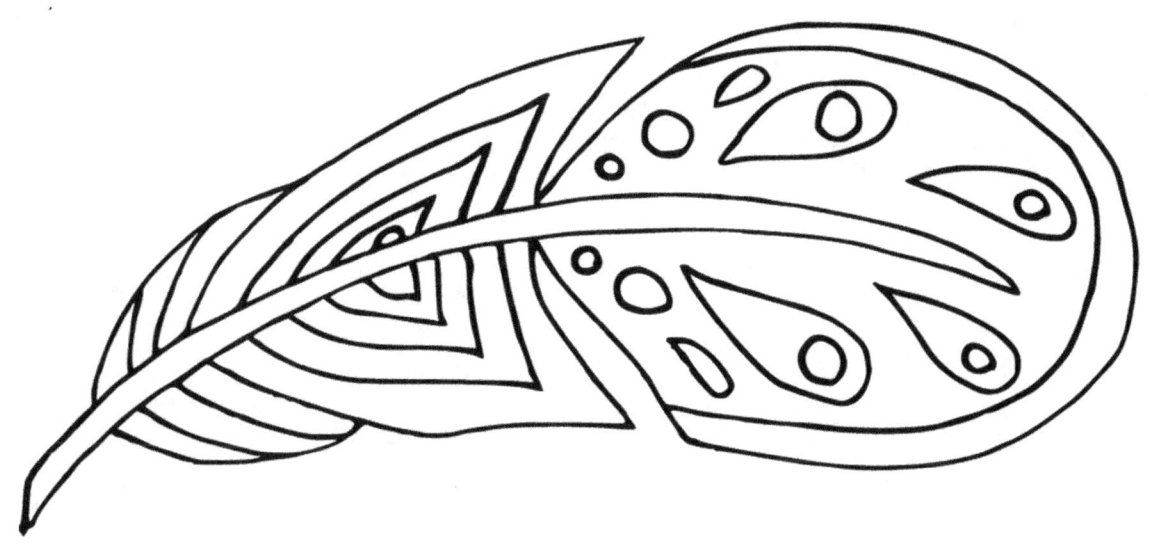

Colorist Palette Reference Book © Ligia Ortega - ColoringPress.com

Colorist Palette Reference Book © Ligia Ortega - ColoringPress.com

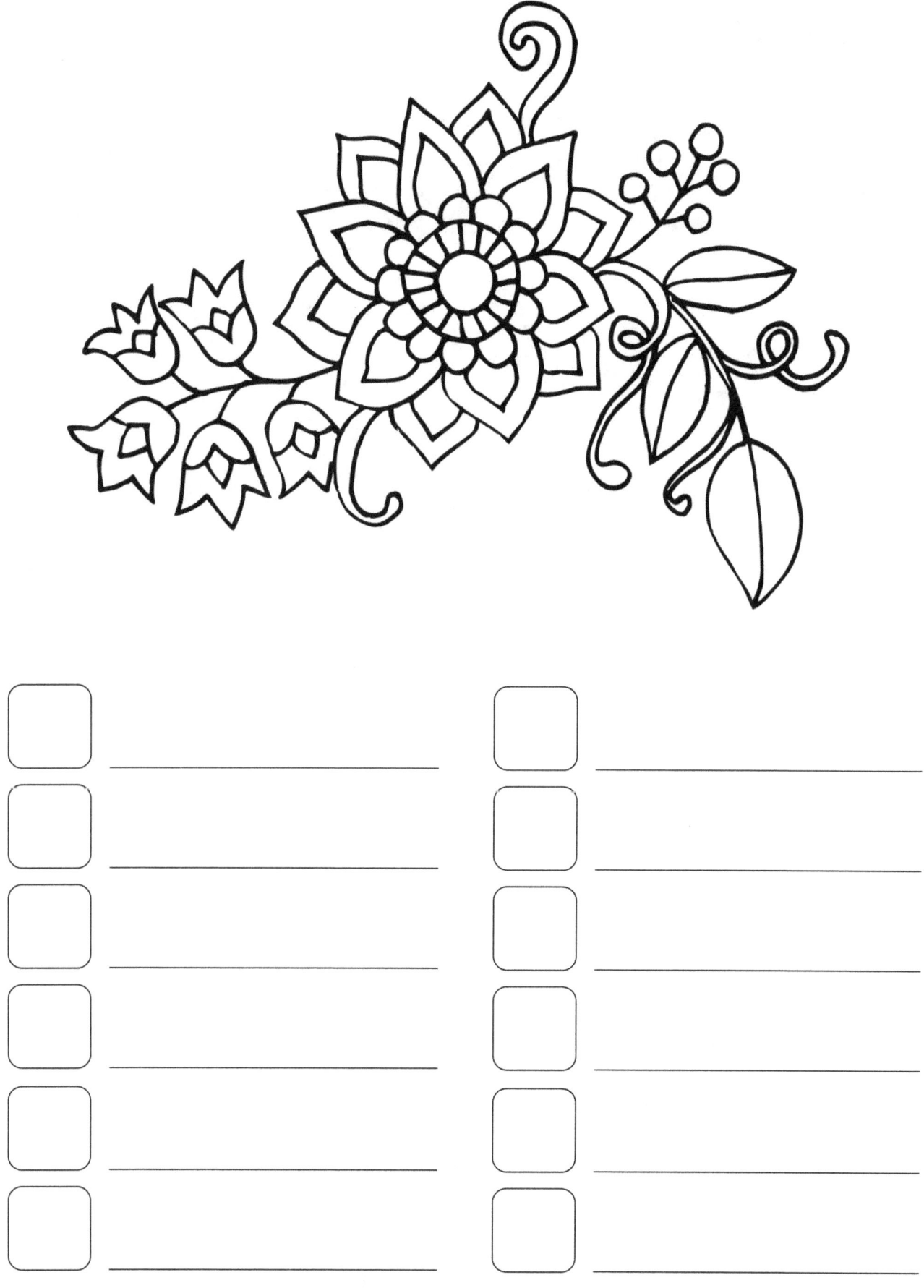

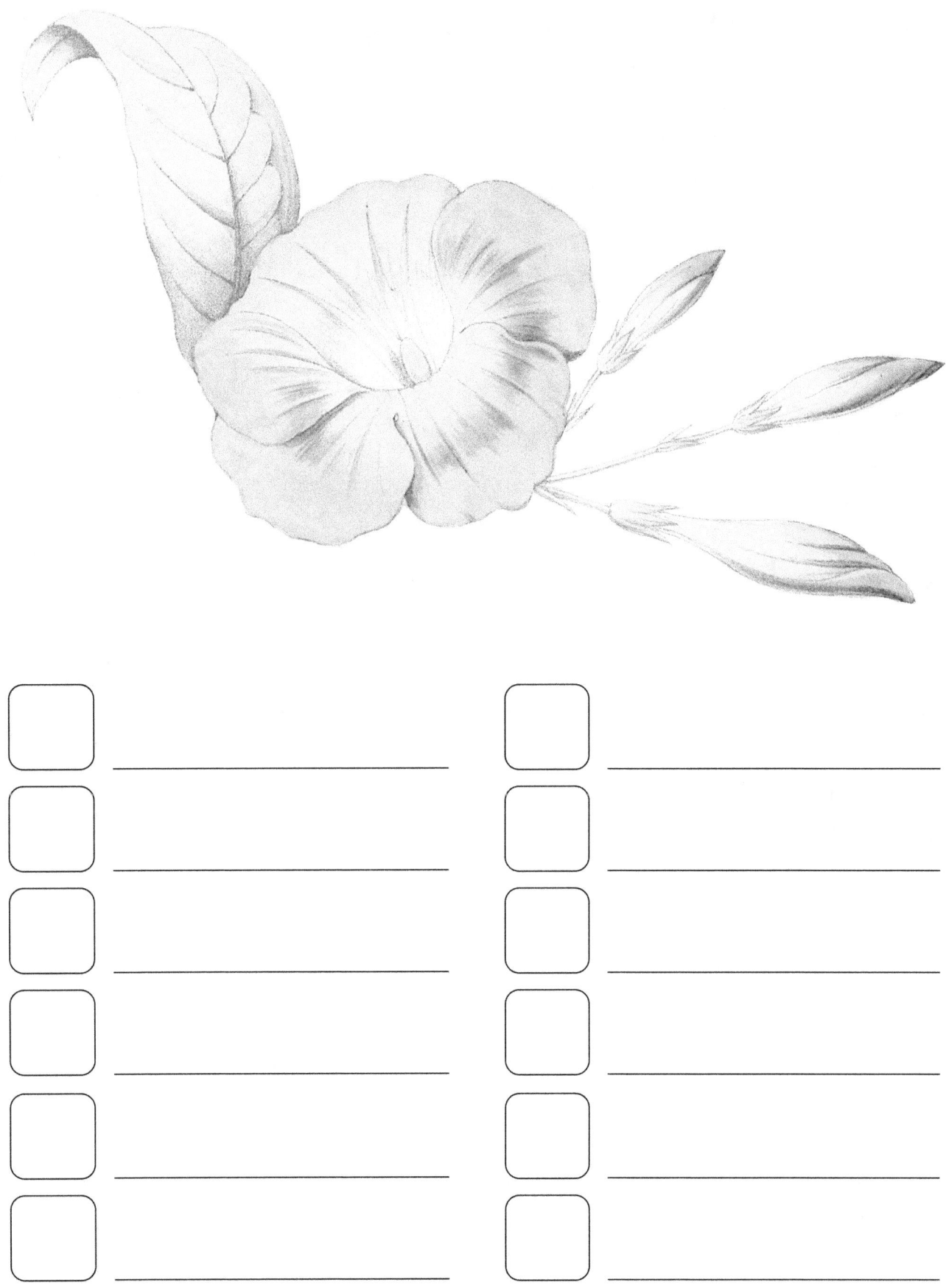

Colorist Palette Reference Book © Ligia Ortega - ColoringPress.com

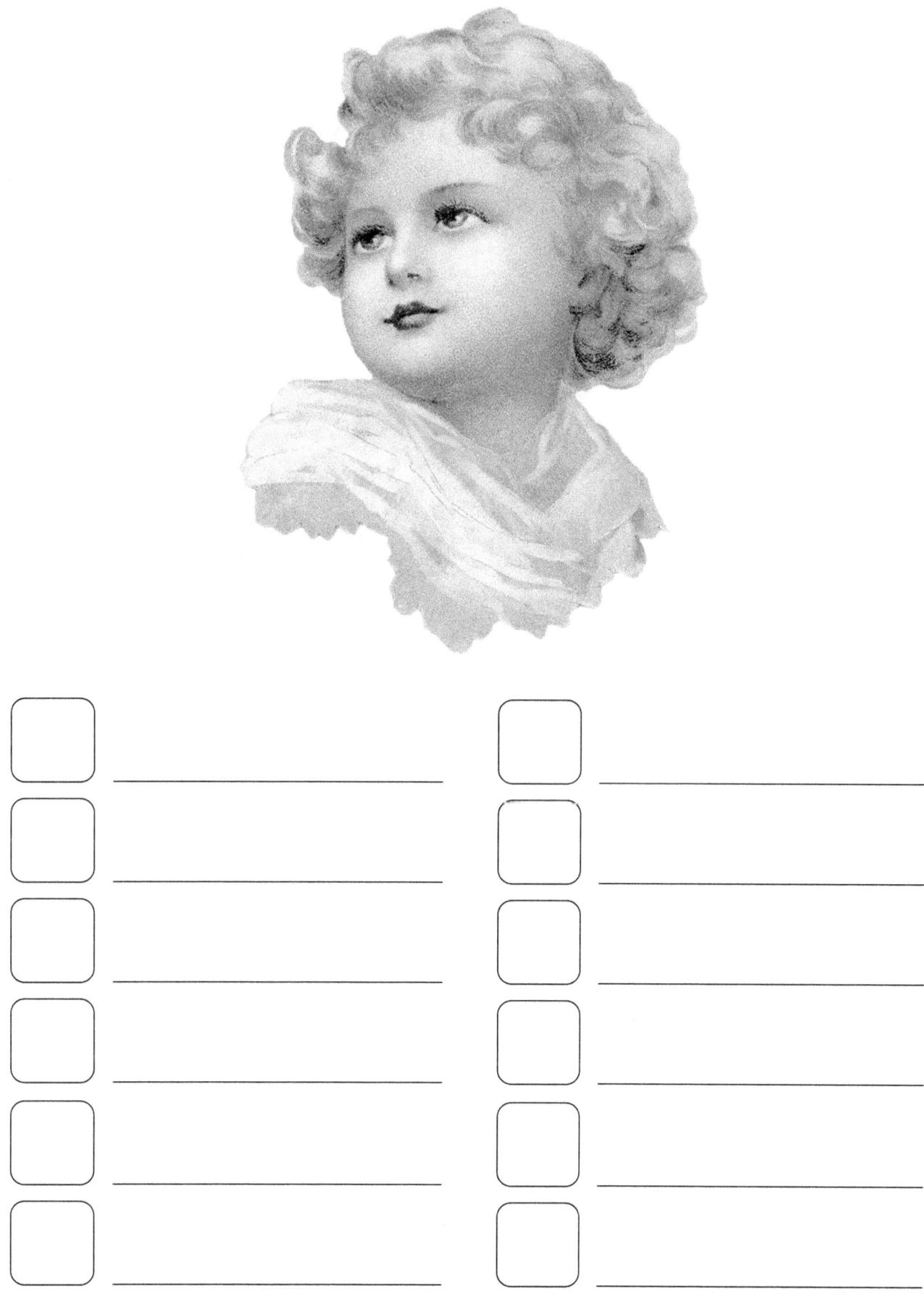

Colorist Palette Reference Book © Ligia Ortega - ColoringPress.com

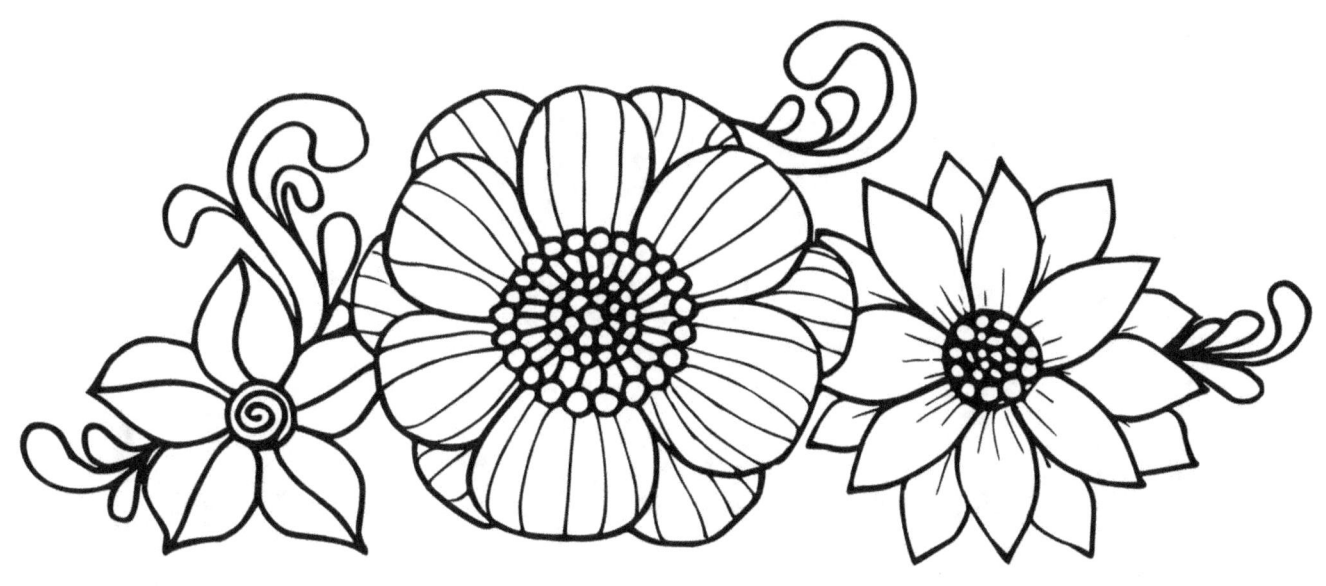

Colorist Palette Reference Book © Ligia Ortega - ColoringPress.com

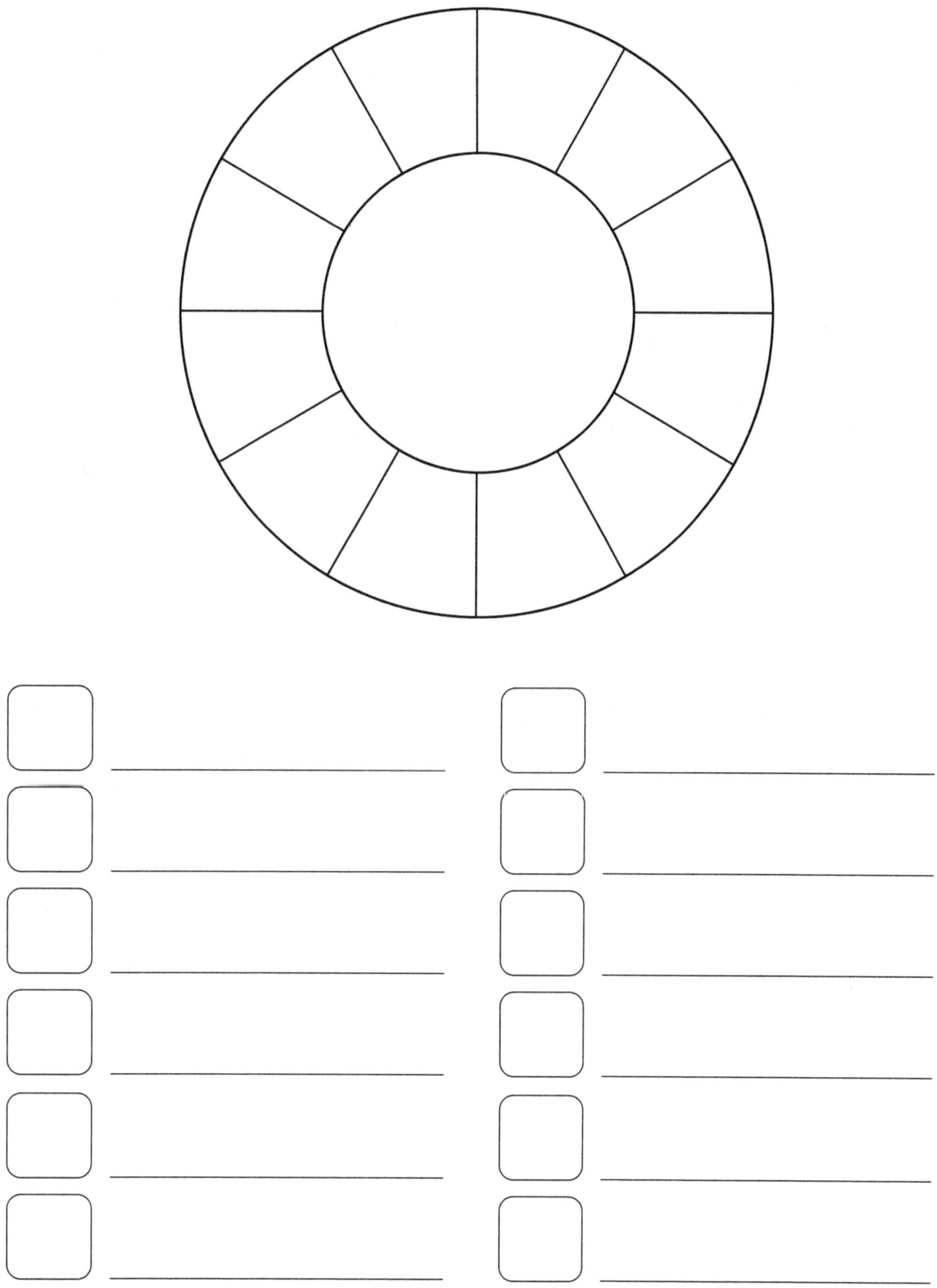

Colorist Palette Reference Book © Ligia Ortega - ColoringPress.com

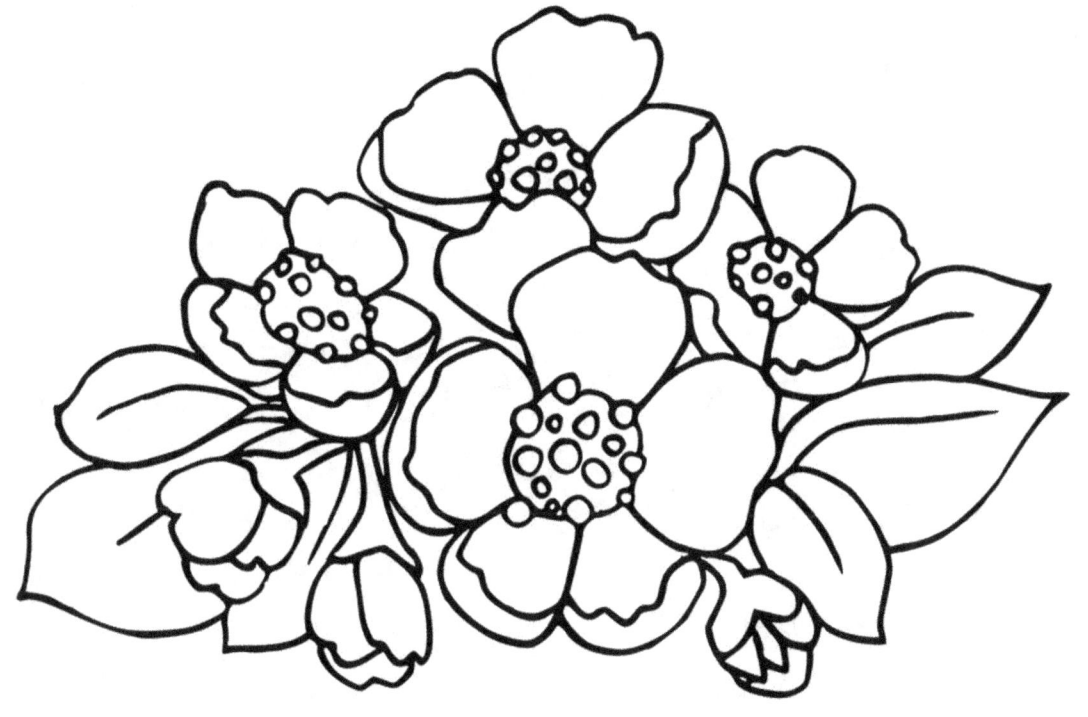

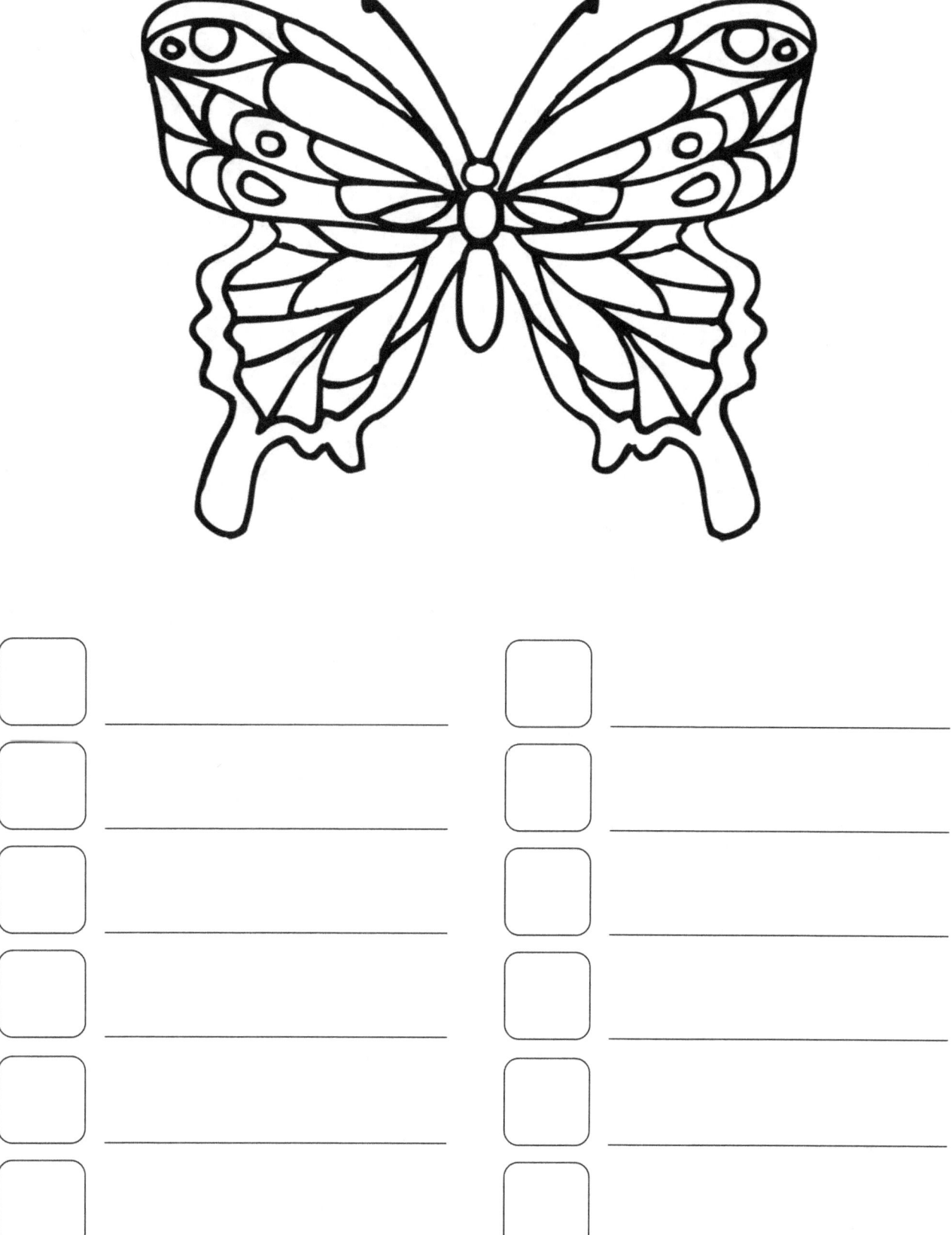

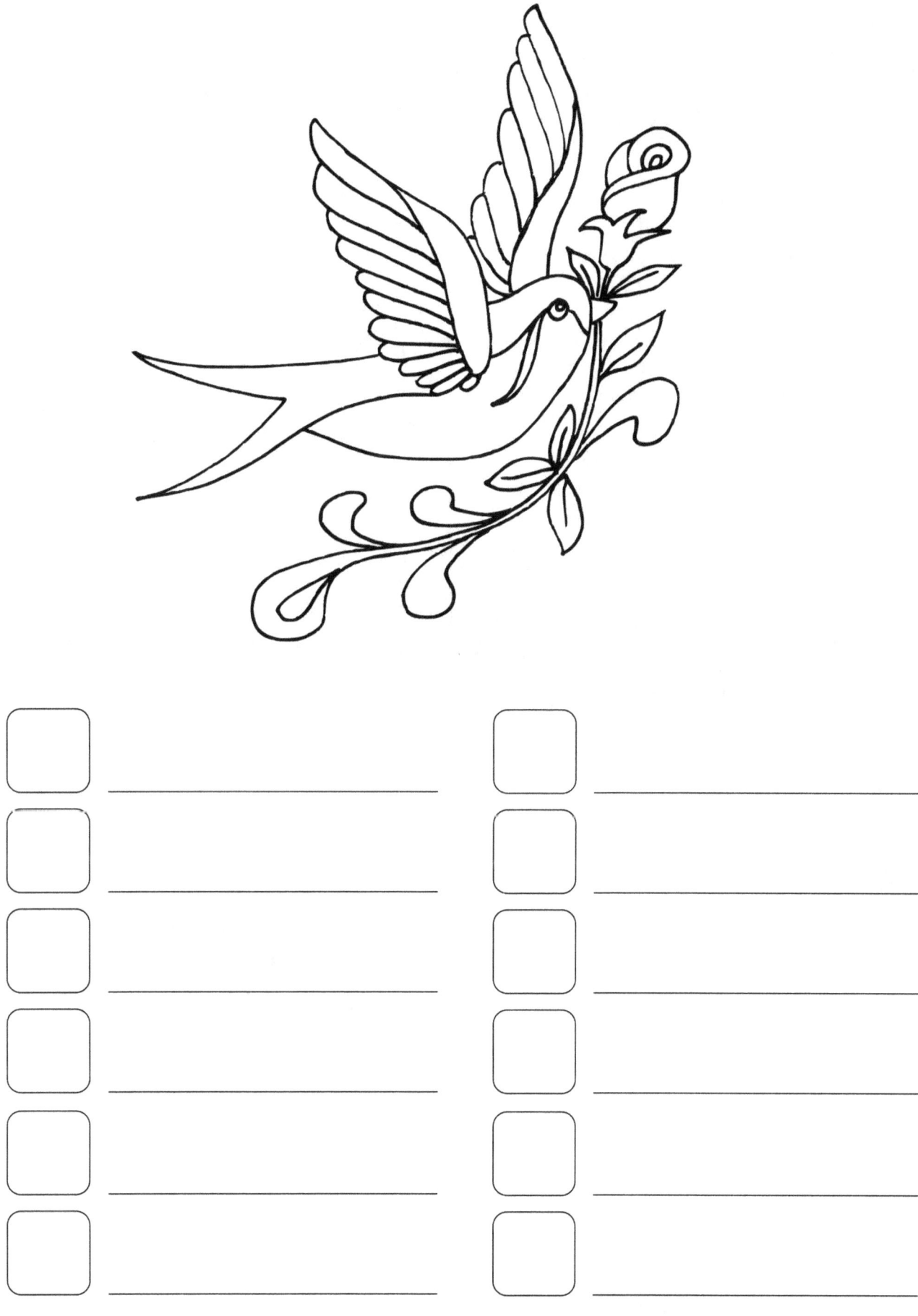

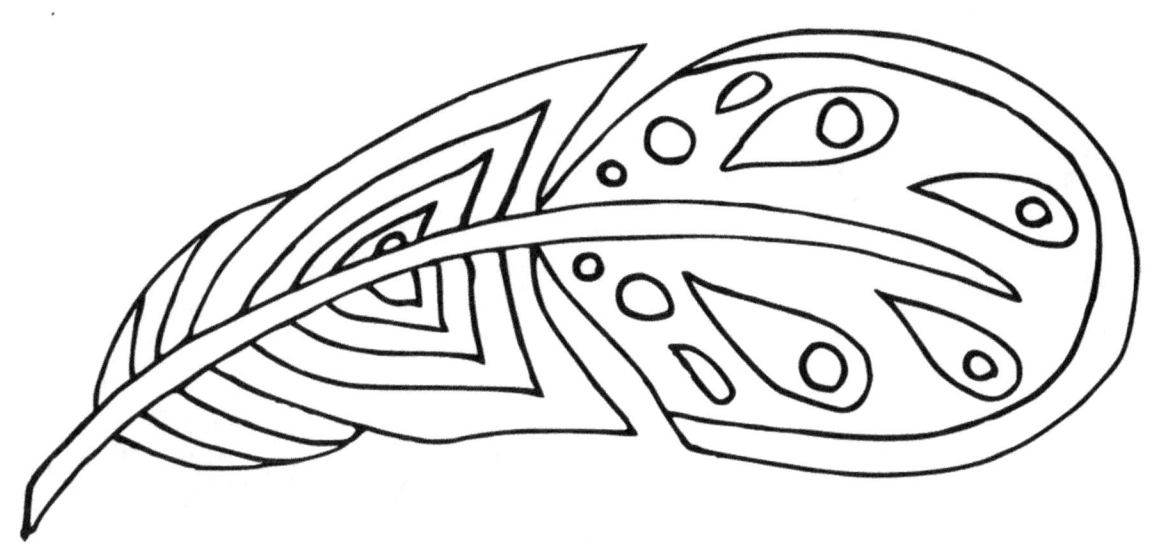

Colorist Palette Reference Book © Ligia Ortega - ColoringPress.com

Colorist Palette Reference Book © Ligia Ortega - ColoringPress.com

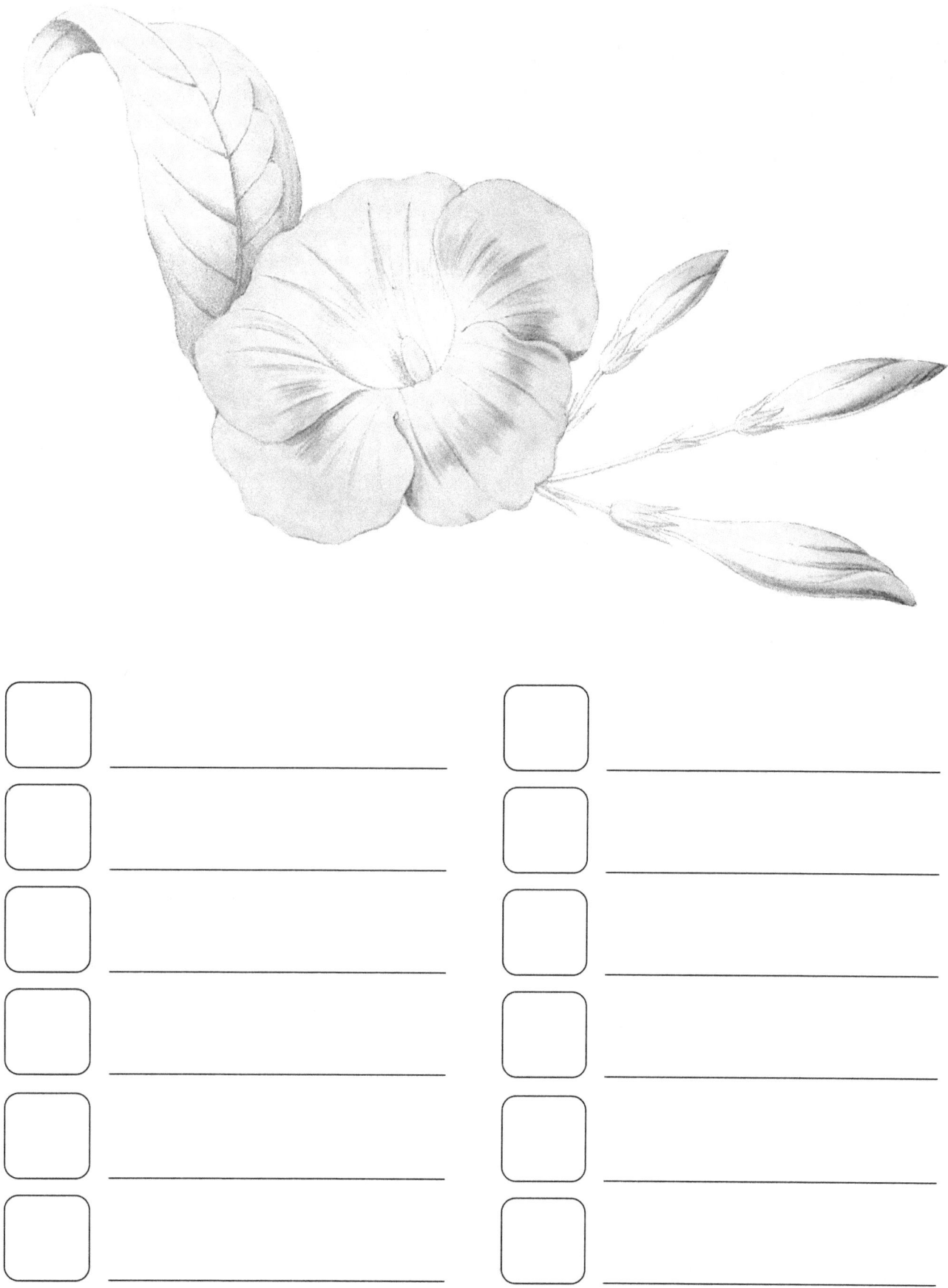

Colorist Palette Reference Book © Ligia Ortega - ColoringPress.com

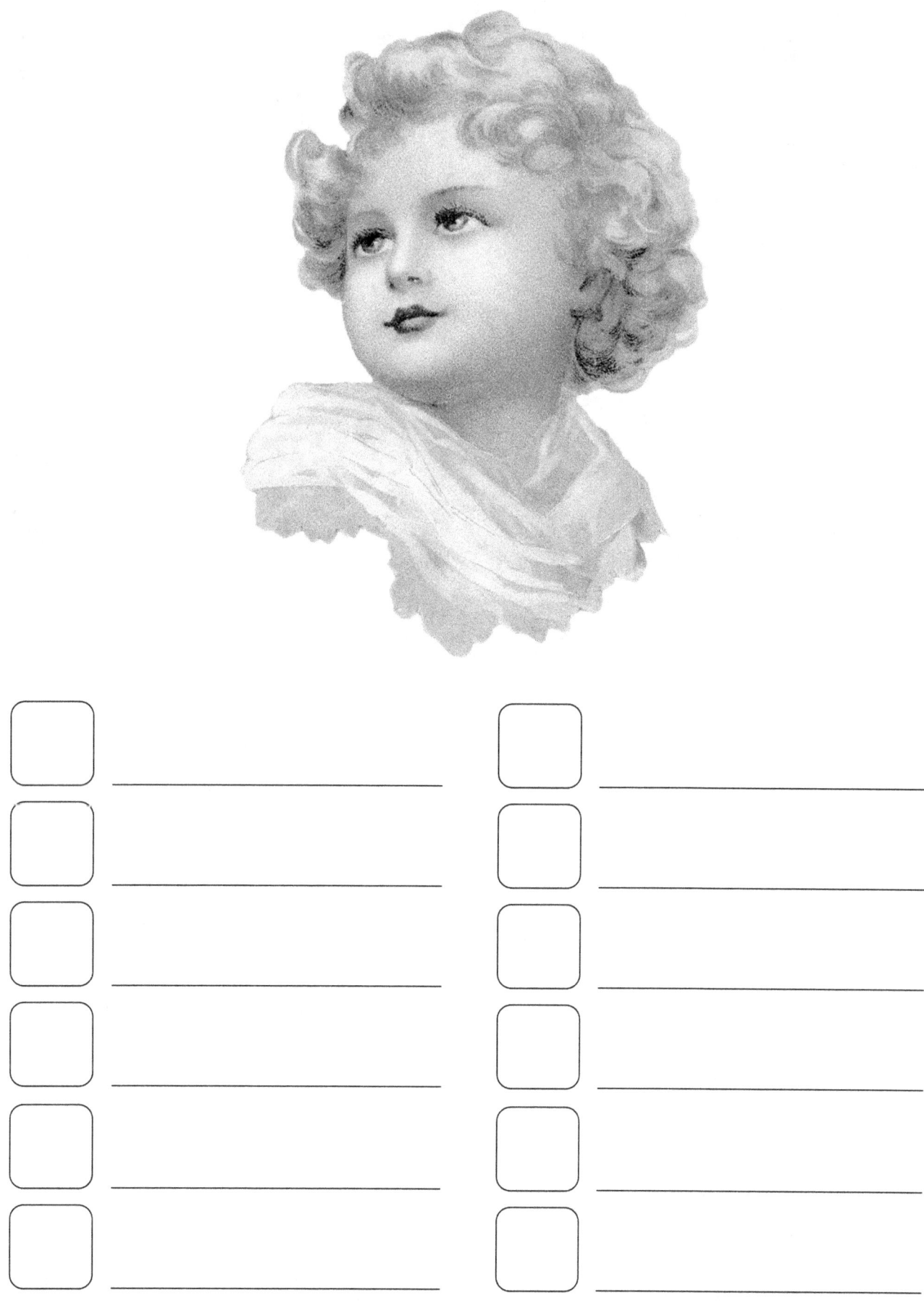

Colorist Palette Reference Book © Ligia Ortega - ColoringPress.com

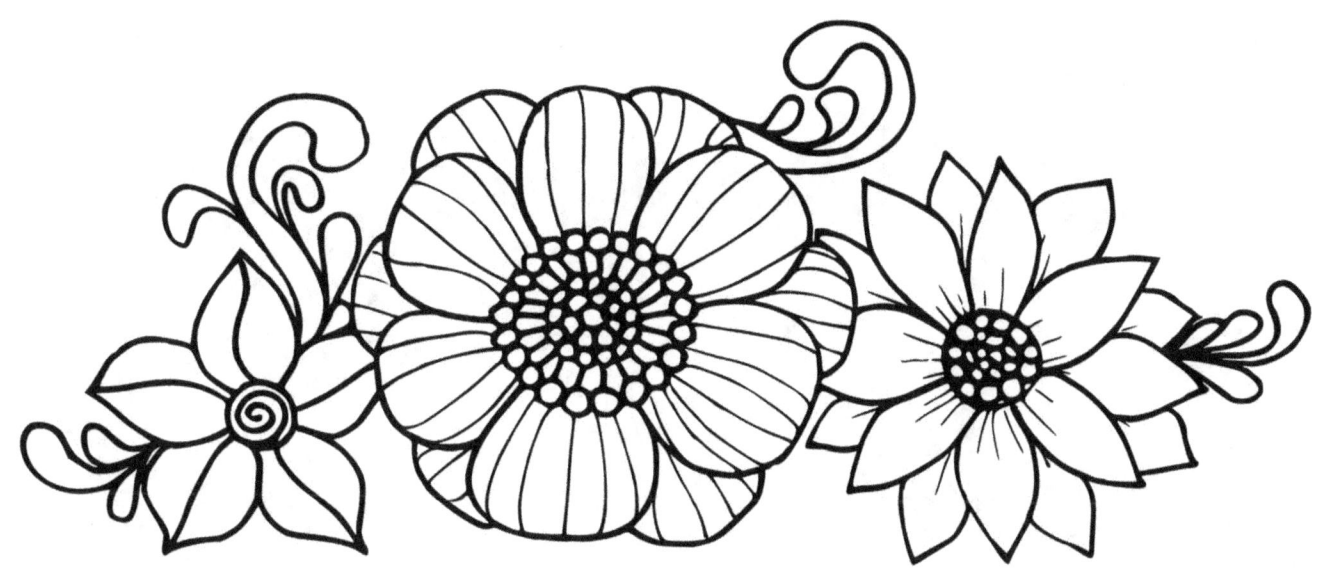

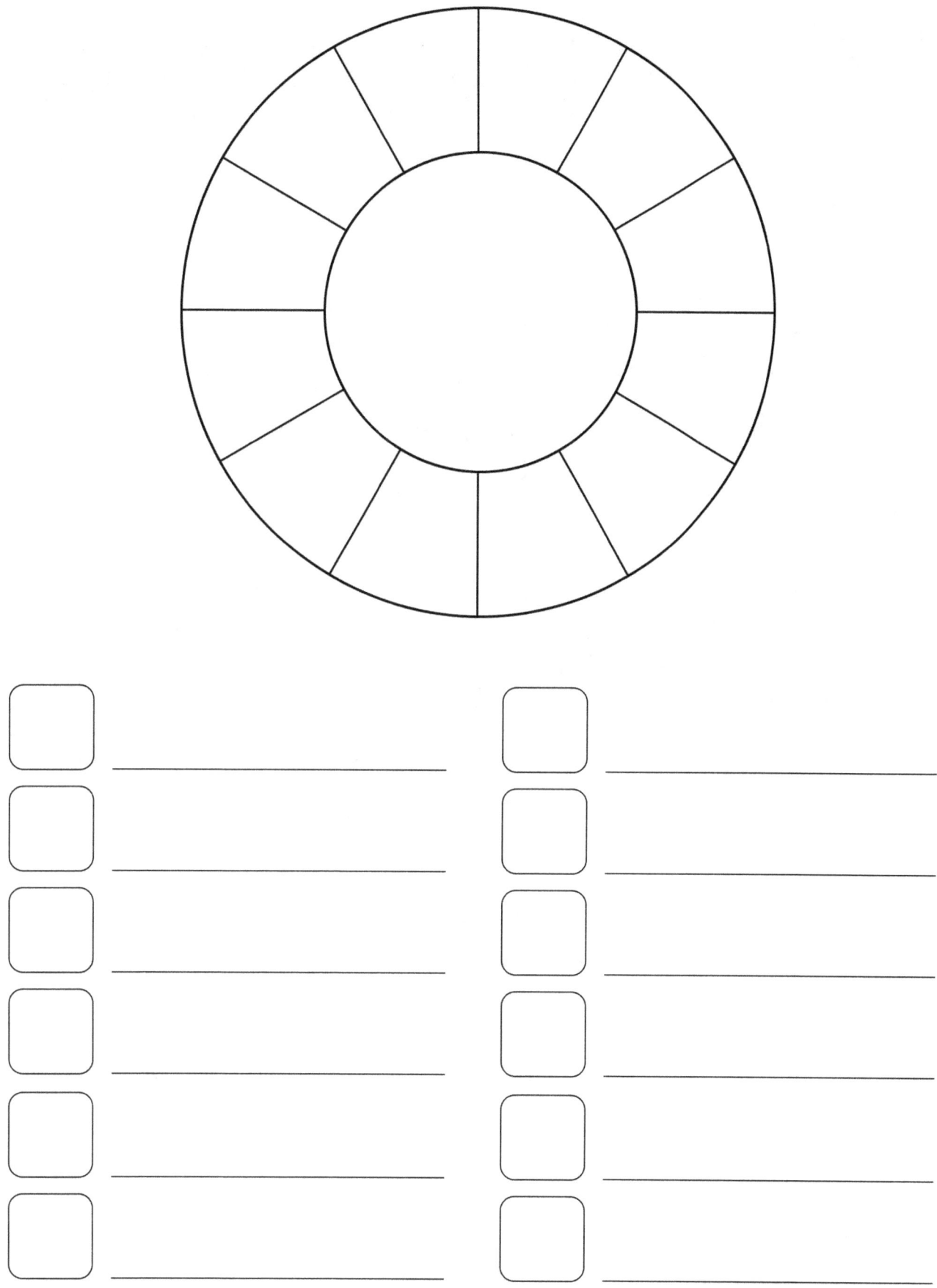

Colorist Palette Reference Book © Ligia Ortega - ColoringPress.com

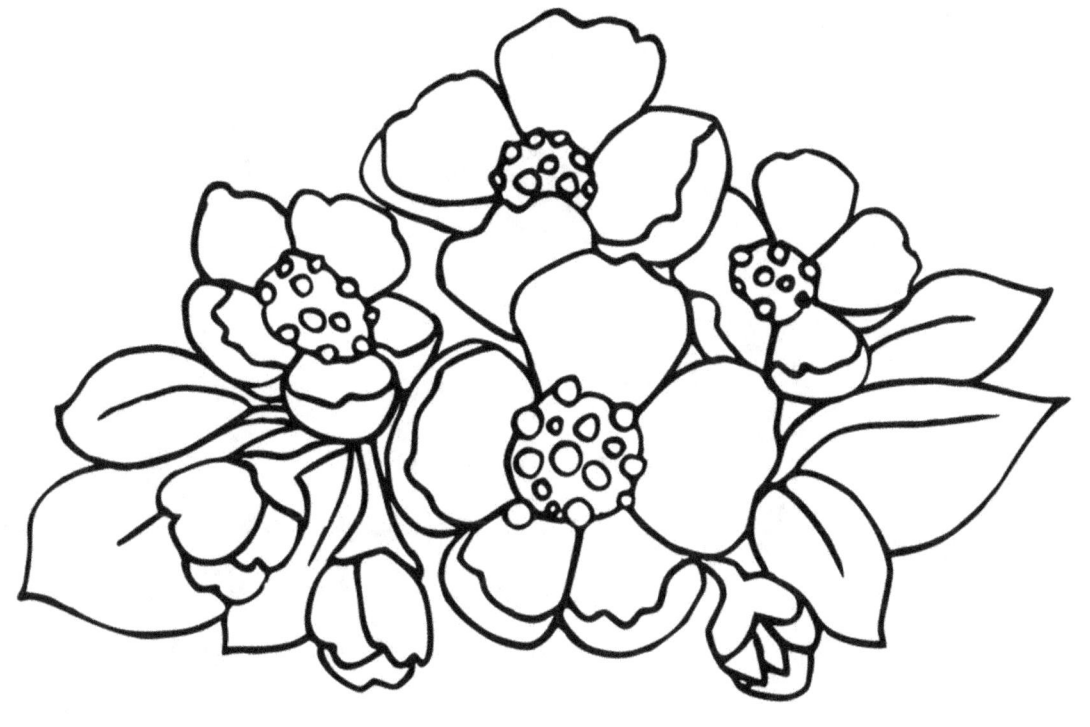

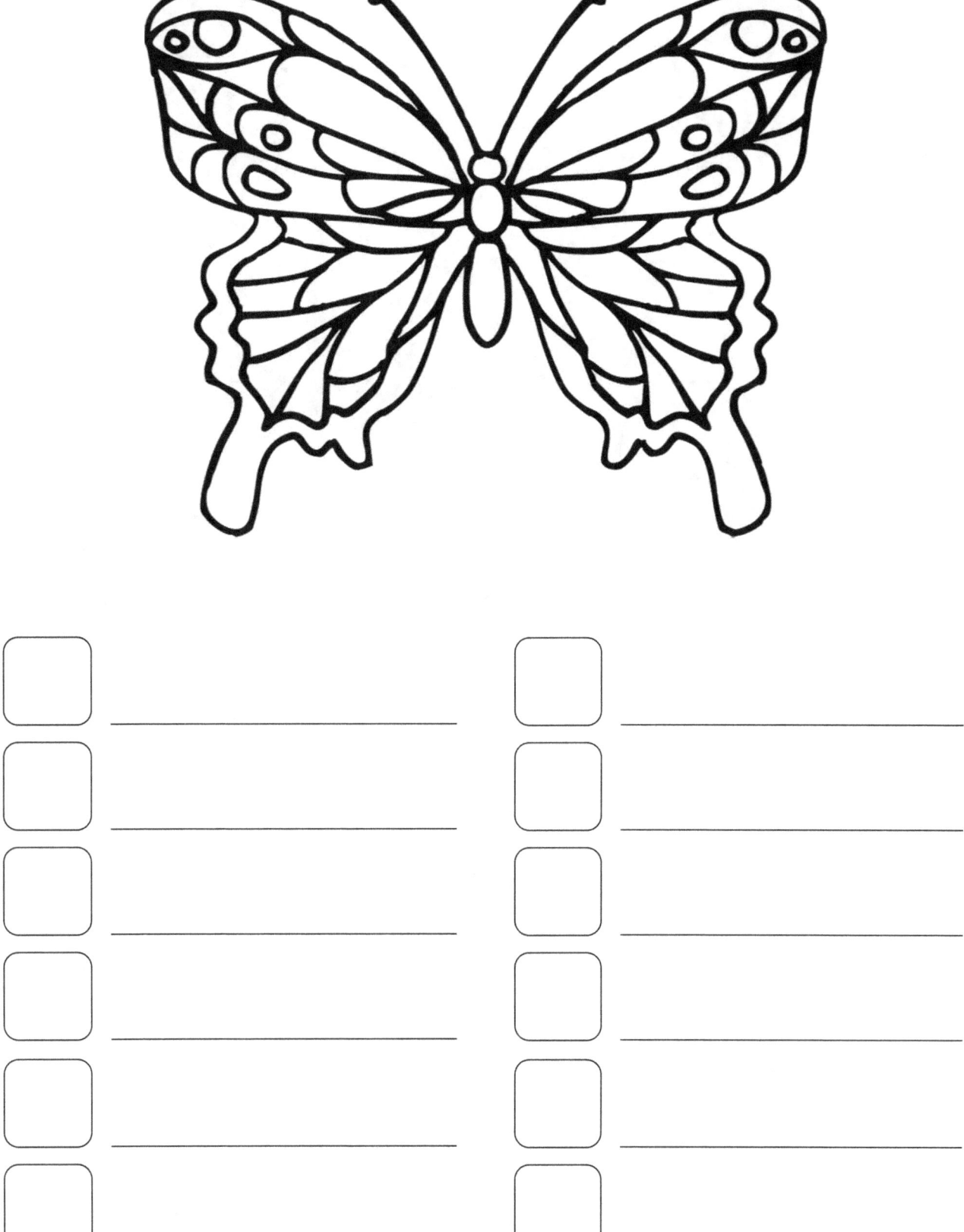

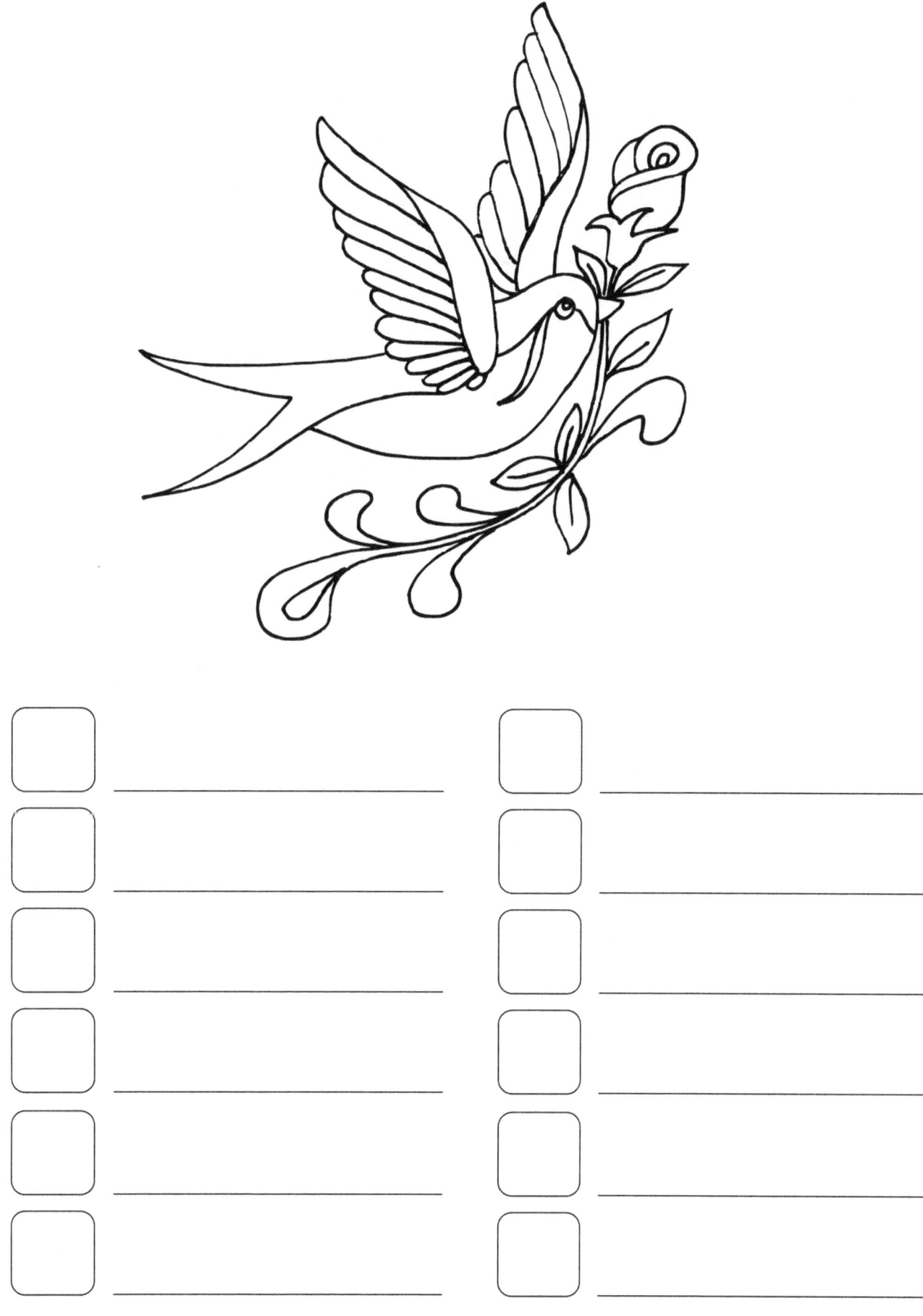

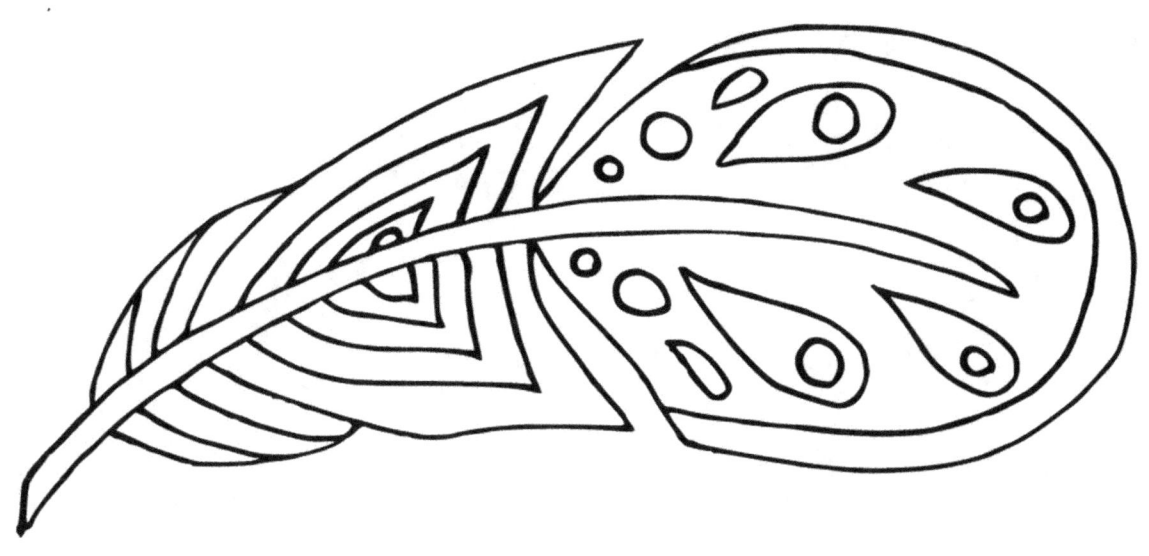

Colorist Palette Reference Book © Ligia Ortega - ColoringPress.com

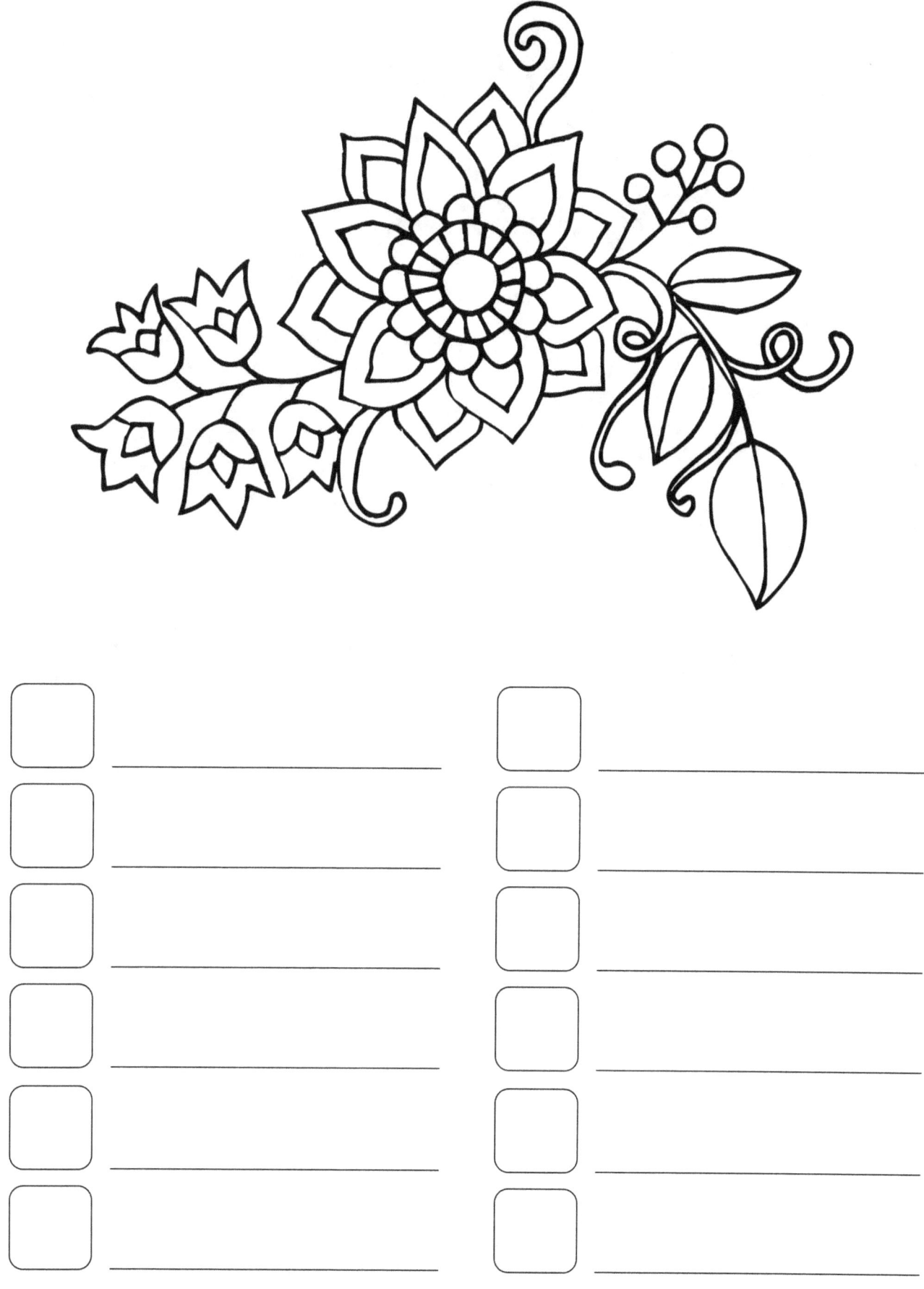

Colorist Palette Reference Book © Ligia Ortega - ColoringPress.com

Colorist Palette Reference Book © Ligia Ortega - ColoringPress.com

Colorist Palette Reference Book © Ligia Ortega - ColoringPress.com

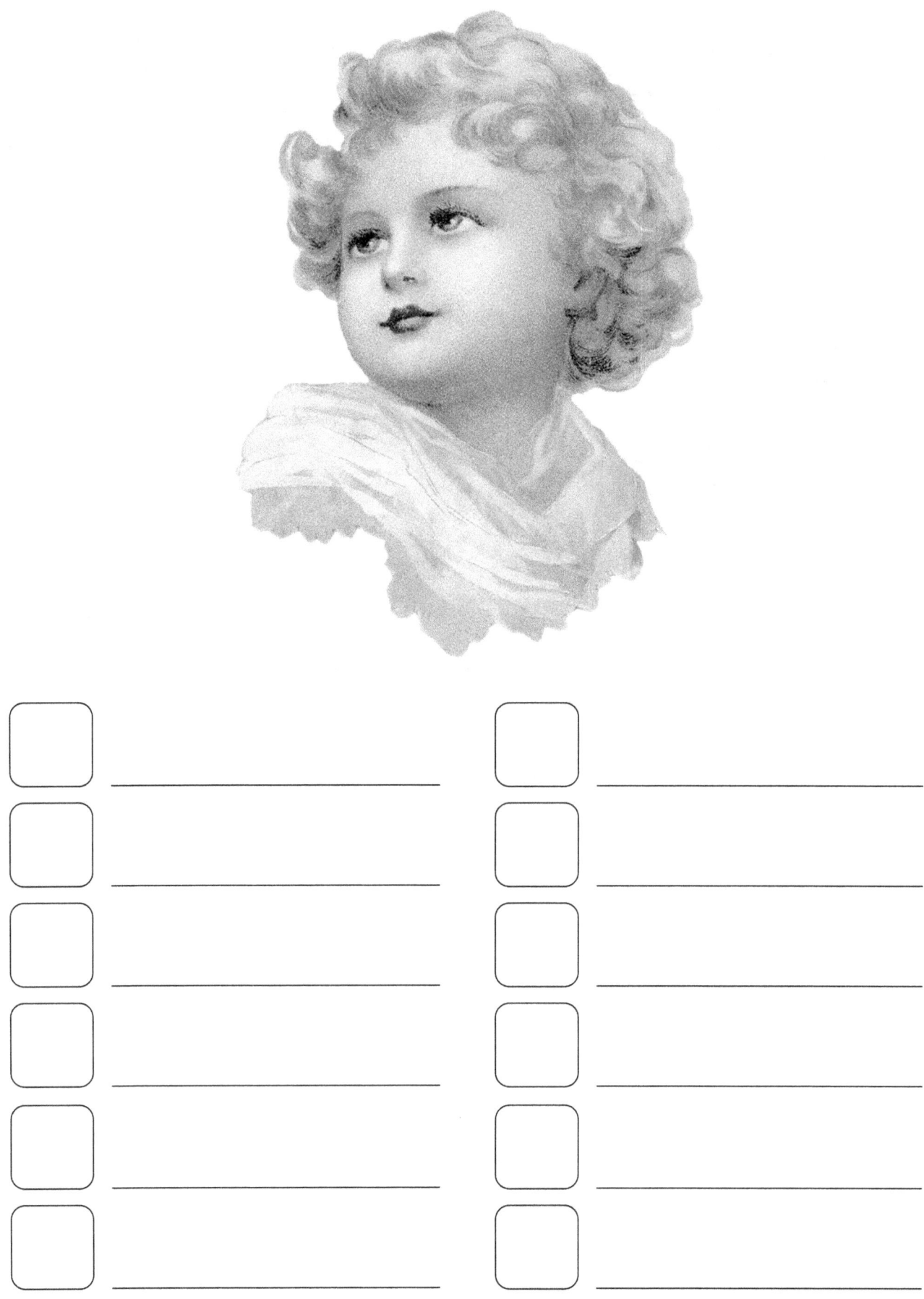

Colorist Palette Reference Book © Ligia Ortega - ColoringPress.com

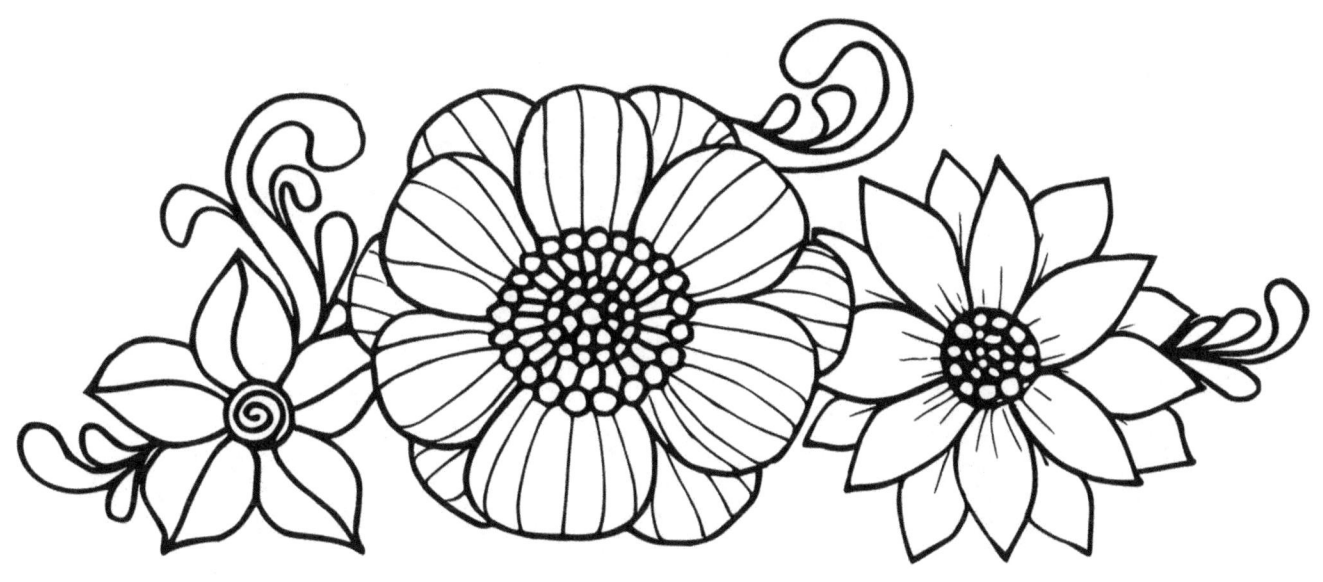

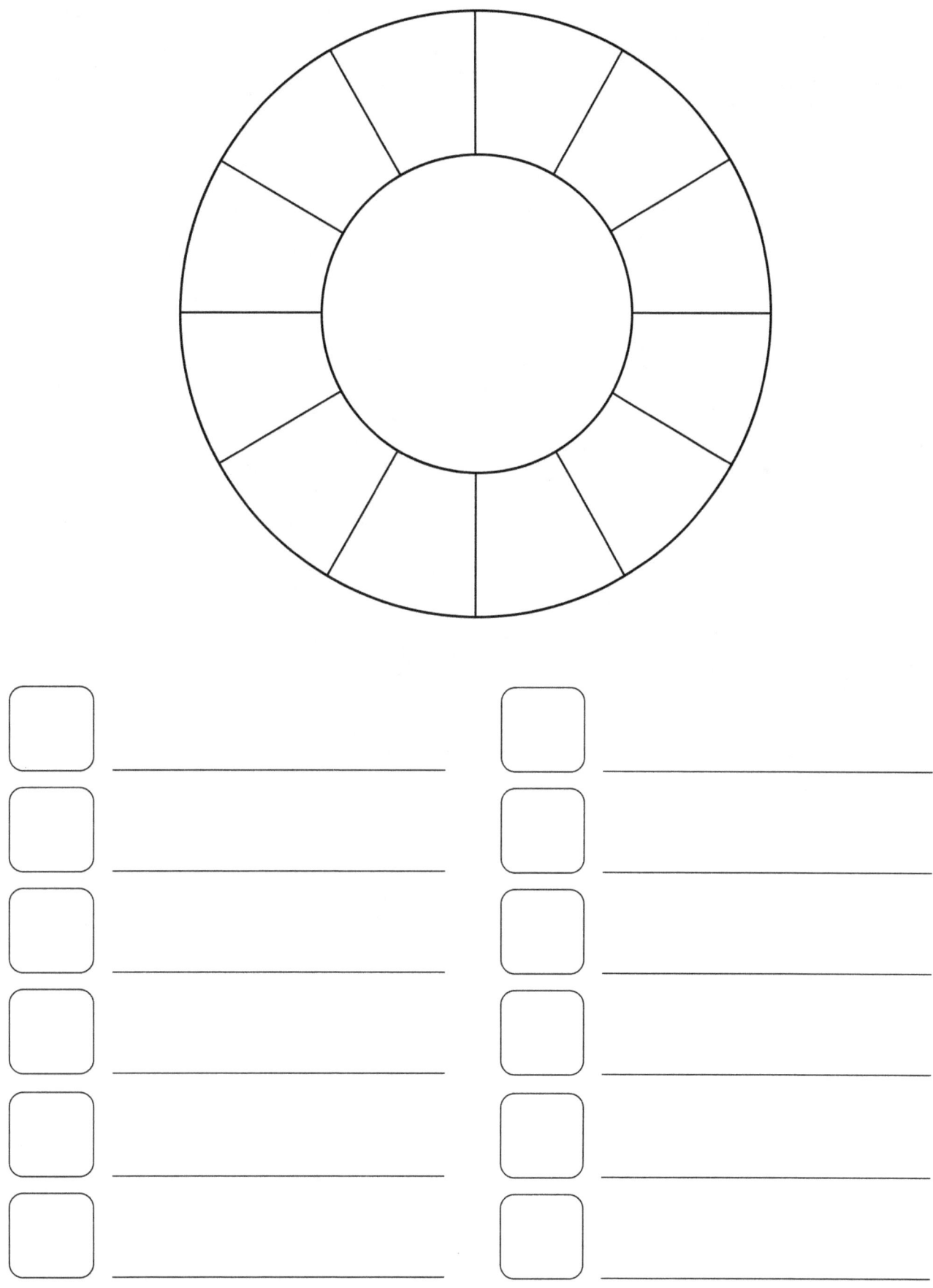

Colorist Palette Reference Book © Ligia Ortega - ColoringPress.com

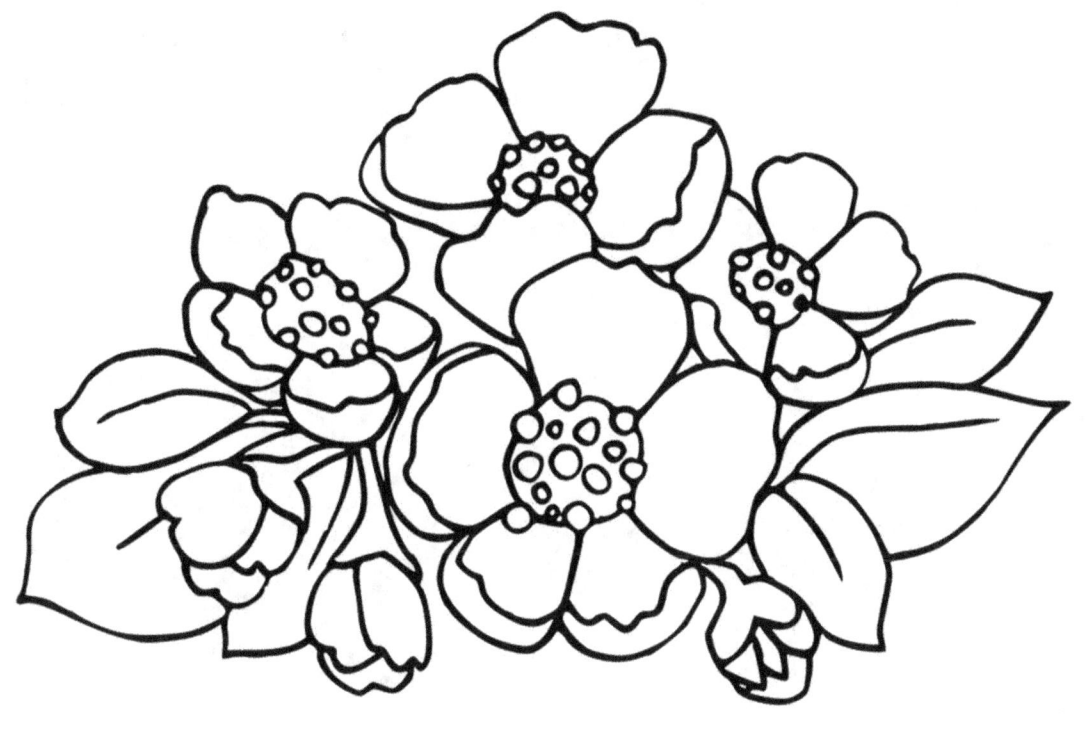

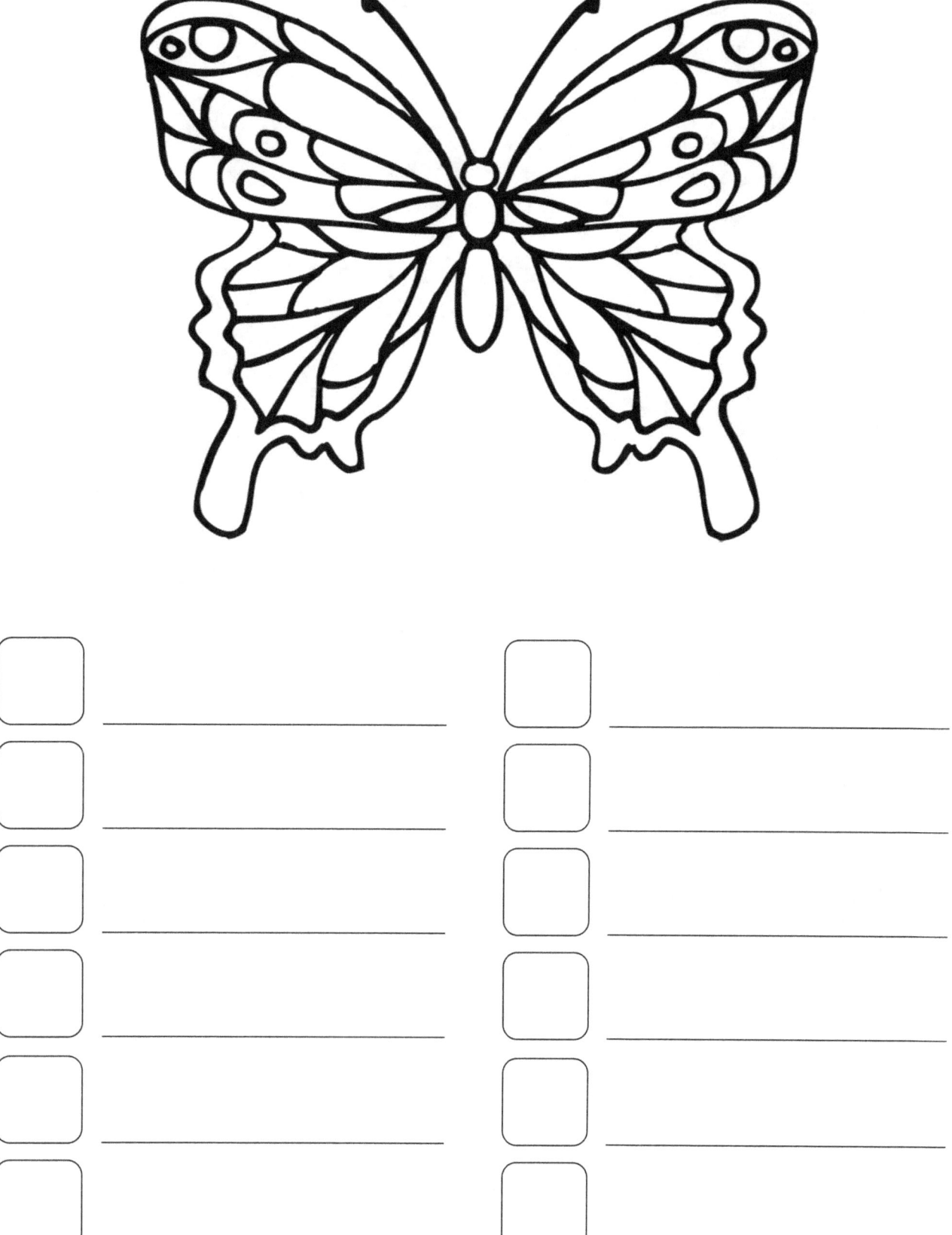

Colorist Palette Reference Book © Ligia Ortega - ColoringPress.com

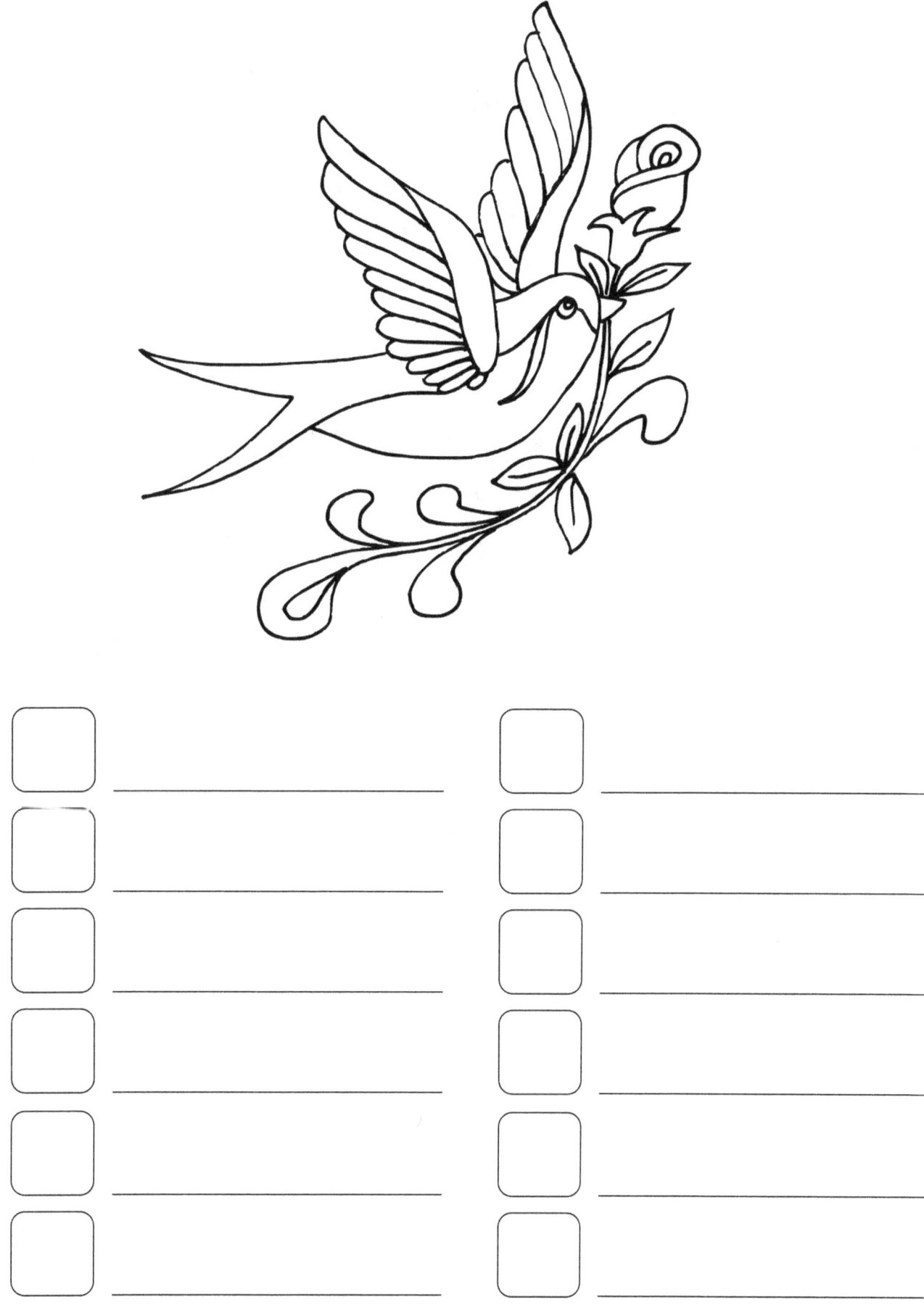

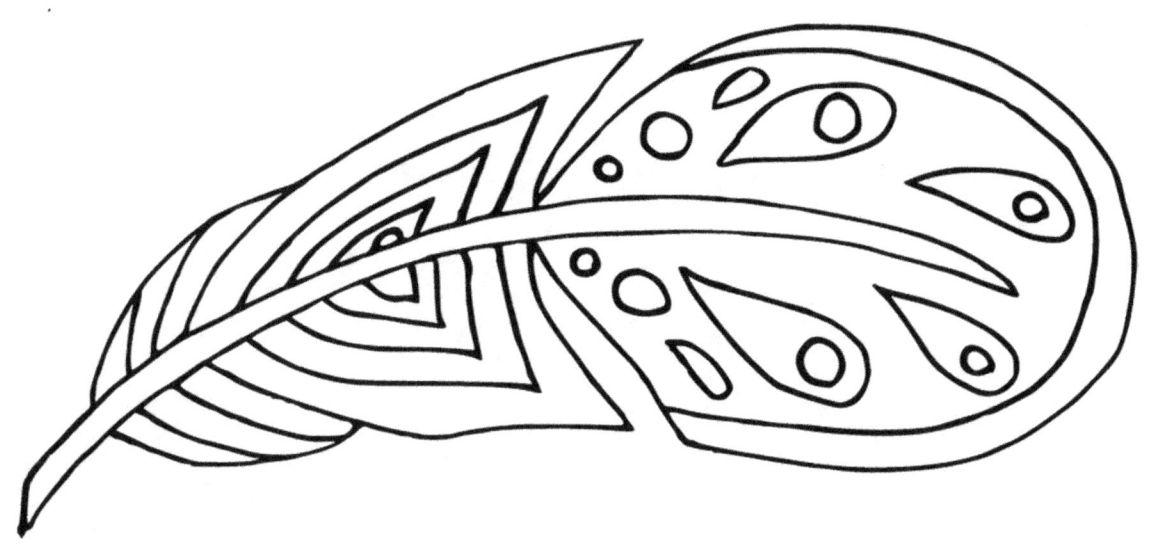

Colorist Palette Reference Book © Ligia Ortega - ColoringPress.com

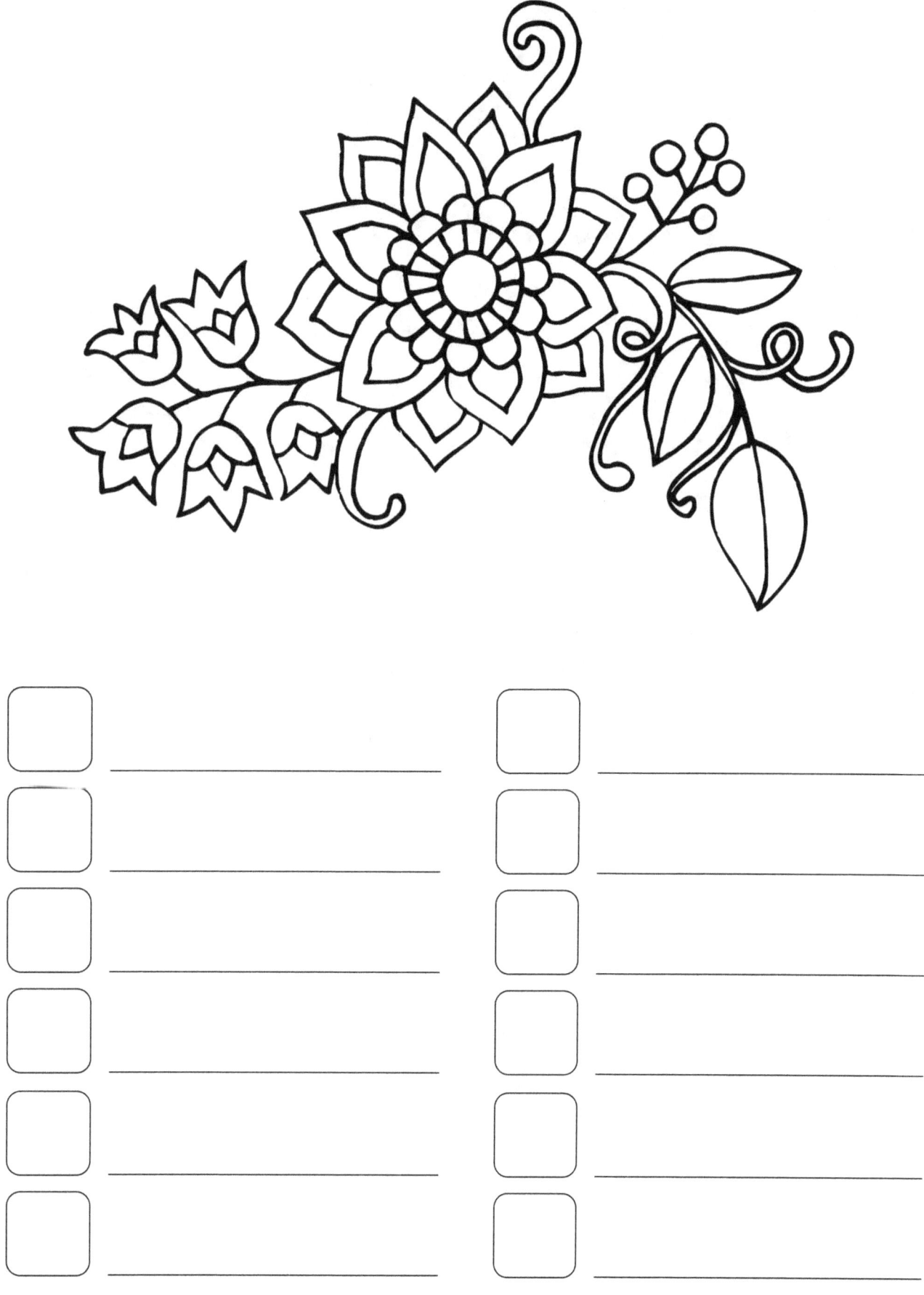

Colorist Palette Reference Book © Ligia Ortega - ColoringPress.com

Colorist Palette Reference Book © Ligia Ortega - ColoringPress.com

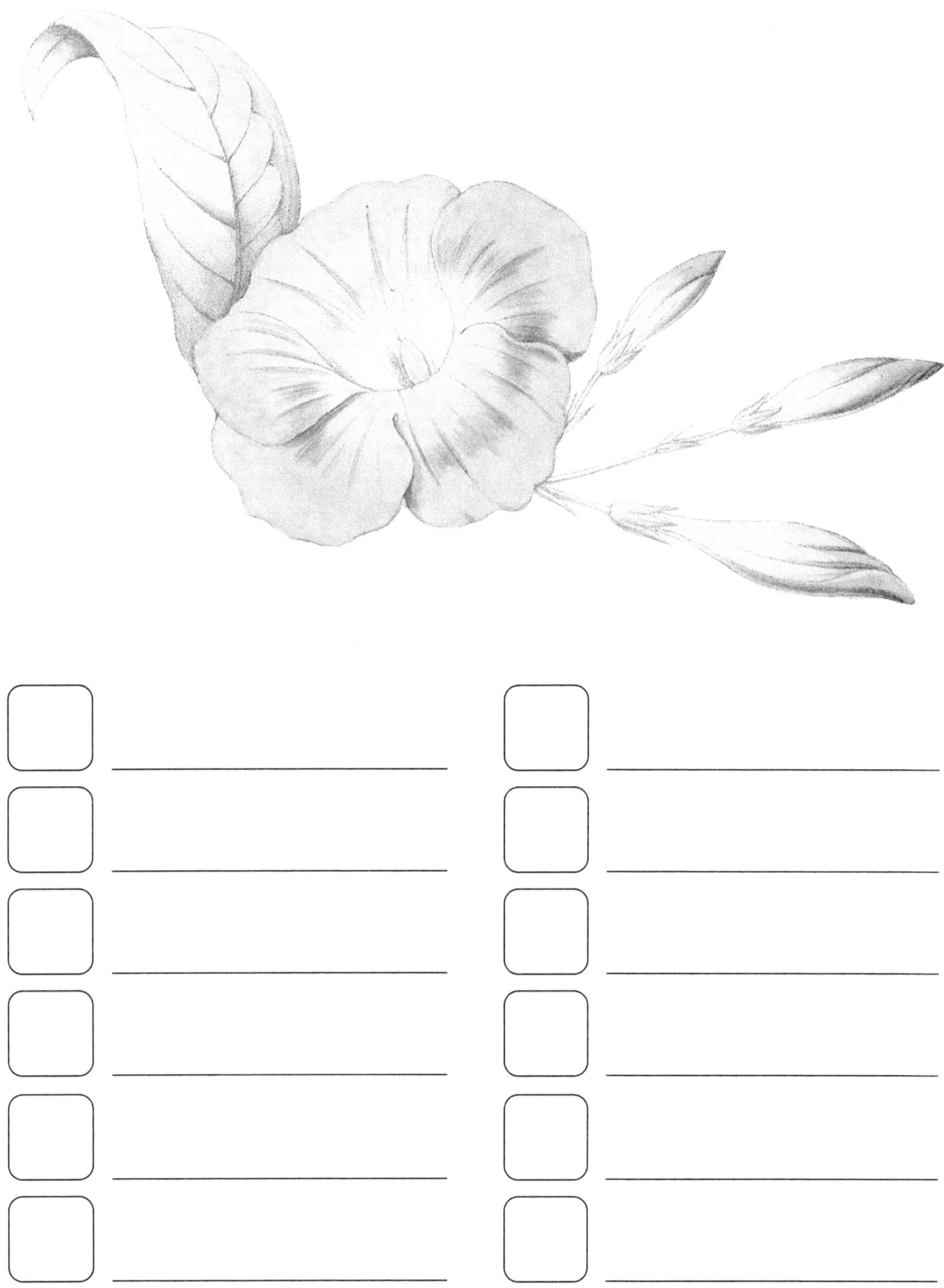

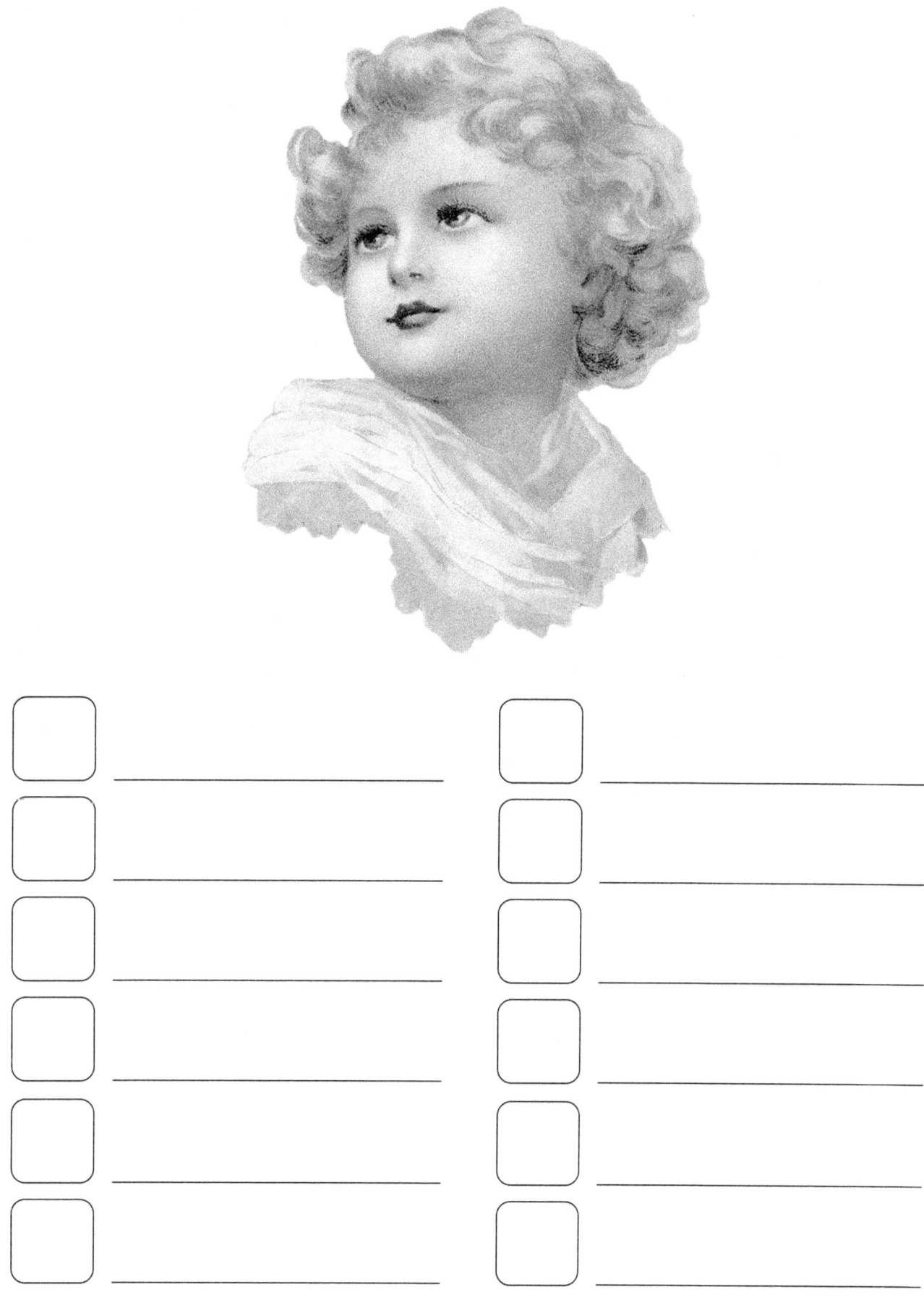

Colorist Palette Reference Book © Ligia Ortega - ColoringPress.com

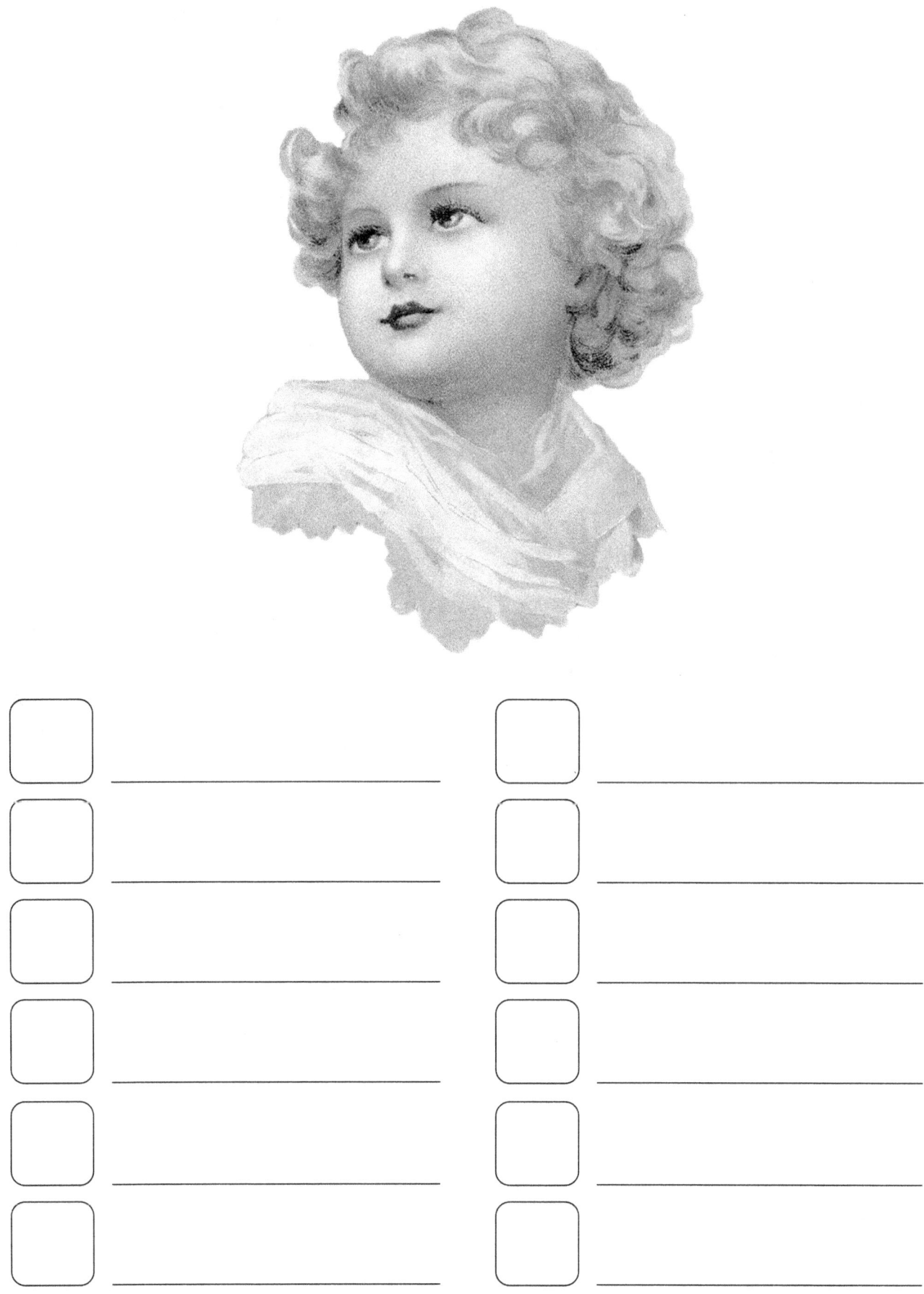

I hope you found the Colorist Palette Reference Book useful!

Please take a moment to leave a review on the book's Amazon book page.

To Find:

- Coloring tips
- Grayscale coloring information
- My Coloring Gifts™ book series
- My Vintage Grayscale book series
- My Simple Designs book series
- Journals, Electronic Downloads
- My blog and to sign up for my email newsletter
- Coloring Press on Facebook, Instagram, and other social media

Please visit my site at **ColoringPress.com**

www.ingramcontent.com/pod-product-compliance
Lightning Source LLC
Chambersburg PA
CBHW082346220526
45470CB00008B/2666